*This book is dedicated
to our loyal
Delicious! Magazine
readers.*

New Hope Communications Inc.
1301 Spruce Street
Boulder, Colorado 80302

Copyright @ 1994 by New Hope Communications Inc.

All rights reserved. No part of this publication may be reproduced, stored in a retrieval system, or transmitted, in any form or by any means, electronic, mechanical, photocopying, recording, or otherwise, without the prior written permission of the publisher.

Frederick, Sue
How to shop a natural foods store –and why / by Sue E. Frederick and Michael Whiteman-Jones.
       p. cm.
   Includes index.
   ISBN 0-9632623-1-9: 5.95 (pbk.)
    1. Natural foods–United States. 2. Marketing (Home economics)–United States. 3. Natural foods industry–United States.
I. Whiteman-Jones, Michael. II. Title.
TX369.F74   1994
641.3'02'0973--dc20   93-50187
                                        CIP

Designed by Linda Nussbaum
Illustrations by Matt Foster
Cover Echinacea illustration by Lamya Deeb
Printed in the United States of America

How to Shop
a Natural
Foods Store...
AND WHY

Sue Frederick and Michael Whiteman-Jones
New Hope Communications, Boulder, CO.

Before beginning any health program, it's best to consult
with a health care professional. The information contained in this book
is not meant to replace the advice of your physician.

Contents

1 SUPPLEMENTS:
From minerals to multivitamins here's all you need to know when shopping for nutritional supplements.

2 HERBS:
Your guide to nature's botanical remedies such as echinacea and goldenseal.

3 PERSONAL CARE: Answers to all your questions about natural personal care products and how to use them.

4 ORGANICS:
What's good for the environment is good for you. Here's why you should buy organic products.

5 Bulk Foods:
Our helpful charts will guide you in selecting and cooking everything from beans to rice to grains.

6 Meat & Dairy:
Why is it better to buy meat and dairy products in a natural foods store? We've got the answers.

7 Soyfoods:
From tofu to tempeh here's how to use soy products and improve your health.

8 Household Products:
Your home should be as free from toxic chemicals as possible.

INTRODUCTION

How Natural Foods are Changing the Way America Views its Health

The natural foods industry has come a long way since it was founded more than 130 years ago. In fact, it doesn't call itself the natural foods industry anymore. Now it's the natural **products** industry. The name change came about a few years ago when industry leaders wanted to acknowledge their inventory not only of fresh, packaged and pre-prepared foods, but of other natural products as well, from clothing made with organically grown cotton to environmentally friendly household cleaners and plant-based medicines.

Many products are well-known; however, others may be unfamiliar. To help consumers in selecting the many new products offered in natural products stores, the editors of *Delicious! Magazine* created *How To Shop A Natural Foods Store And Why*. Each chapter takes you on a step-by-step walk through a typical natural foods store from the produce department to dietary supplements, introducing you to products, laying out the health, environmental and economic benefits of certain products and explaining their history and manufacture. We hope our guide takes some of the mystery out of natural products and enhances your shopping experience — naturally!

Americans began talking about health reform in the early 1800s, when groups of forward-thinking people called for a return to simpler, natural foods that are better for our minds and bodies. One of the earliest proponents of health foods was the Rev. Sylvester Graham, a Presbyterian minister who invented the graham cracker. He preached against meat and fat and recommended a diet rich in fresh, unprocessed whole foods and brans. Graham's formula for health was inspired more by religious fanaticism than nutritional expertise. He believed eating meat promoted promiscuity and condiments caused insanity. However, he also maintained that white bread damaged the digestion and lobbied on behalf of eating unprocessed bread — an idea nutritionists support today.

The natural foods movement formally began in 1866 in Battle Creek, Mich. It was there that Ellen White, spiritual leader of the Seventh Day Adventist church, had a vision instructing her to observe and study basic health laws. White responded by opening the Western Health Reform Institute, where patients ate large quantities of graham bread while refraining from meat, salt, spices, smoking and alcohol. Ten years later, White unwittingly set the movement in full motion by hiring John Harvey Kellogg, M.D., who renamed the institute the Battle Creek Sanatorium.

Kellogg and his market-wise brother, Will, soon improved on the sanatorium's bland diet by creating more appealing healthy foods — including a dry, crispy flaked cereal. It was a hit, and more healthy products followed including an early version of granola and nearly 20 meat substitutes made mostly from nuts and wheat gluten. By 1906, Will Kellogg had ventured out on his own and introduced Kellogg's Toasted Cornflakes to mainstream America, which quickly took cereals to heart and made Battle Creek, home to more than 40 breakfast food companies, the cereal capital of the world. Most of these companies' products are no longer considered health foods because they almost always contain added sugar, preservatives and other undesirable ingredients. However, "What Kellogg did was found the first health foods manufacturing company in America," says William Shurtleff, director of the Soyfoods Center in Lafayette, Calif., and a researcher of natural products for more than 15 years. "Battle Creek Foods was the first and most influential health foods company in the world. Its influence was felt worldwide."

By 1938, about 150 health foods stores existed in the United States, according to the trade magazine *Natural Foods Merchandiser*. The number had grown to about 1,000 by 1960, thanks largely to word of mouth and lectures by health food proponents. "People recovering from various illnesses on programs suggested at these lectures would open health food stores themselves," notes Frank Murray, author and former editor of *Health Foods Retailing*, the industry's first trade magazine, founded in 1936.

By 1981, there were some 6,500 health foods stores in the nation and, today, despite competition from conventional supermarkets, it's estimated that there are more than 10,000.

WILL PEOPLE THINK I'M STRANGE FOR EATING NATURAL FOODS?

More people than ever are shopping in natural products stores. One reason is because these stores offer products that supply the needs of health-conscious America. For example a recent survey by Yankelovich Clancy Shulman reveals that nearly half of all Americans regularly take dietary supplements, a popular natural products store item. Another recent study cited in *New England Journal of Medicine* concluded that 34 percent of Americans spent $13.7 billion in 1990 on some form of alternative medicine such as herbalism and homeopathy — all of which require products distributed through natural products stores.

A rapidly growing field of health care is nutritional therapy. No longer is food merely a substance that relieves our hunger pangs. Now food is also the first line of defense in health care (no wonder some experts have dubbed certain foods "nutraceuticals"). This national trend toward healthier lifestyles is influencing mainstream food manufacturers and restaurants—even the Pentagon serves vegetarian meals these days; however, the soul of the movement remains in health products stores.

One measure of the nation's interest in natural foods is sales. Although the price of natural foods can be 10 to 20 percent higher than conventional foods, their sales have steadily risen since 1980, when they approached $2 billion. After growing respectably through the mid-1980s, the industry's sales leaped forward more than 7 percent in 1987 — roughly the same time that consumers learned of the importance of increasing fiber consumption and reducing cholesterol to help prevent cancer and heart disease. Industry sales have continued their dramatic rise ever since, growing at a rate of nearly 10 percent a year even during the nationwide recession in the early 1990s. By comparison, the growth rate in the $376 billion grocery business was only 4.3 percent during the same period. It appears this trend will continue throughout the 1990s and beyond. From 1991 to 1992, the latest years for which statistics are available, sales in the natural products industry climbed from about $4.6 billion to nearly $5.3 billion. That equates to a 13.8 percent increase and is the industry's single biggest jump in 13 years. Meanwhile, sales in the supplement industry are pegged at about $3.3 billion a year, while the American Herbal Products Association says herb sales — excluding cooking herbs such as basil — topped $1 billion last year.

How do I choose a natural products store?

Natural products stores can be found almost everywhere — from our biggest cities to small-town America — and they serve customers from all walks of life.

Each store is as unique as its owner, and it can take a little on-site research to choose one that suits your personality, philosophy and needs. More and more natural foods stores are full-service grocers, which means they sell everything from supplements and bulk beans to fresh meat and vitamins. They often have delis and small restaurants, and they may sell gourmet products that fall outside the traditional definition of health foods — ice cream, pies or white French bread, for instance. Some stores are committed to vegetarianism and sell no meat. Others don't sell anything made with white sugar. Still others emphasize herbs, vitamins and other supplements over foods. A few cater to athletes with special dietary needs.

Chapter 1
SUPPLEMENTS

How to shop for dietary supplements

HISTORY The discovery of vitamins probably dates to the 1700s, when Sir Robert Lind, a Scottish physician in the Royal Navy, discovered he could prevent scurvy in sailors by giving them lime juice (British sailors are sometimes still called "Limeys"). Vitamin research took a major step forward in the late 1800s, when residents of Dutch colonies in East India, who subsisted mainly on white rice, began dying from a disease called beriberi. Scientists studied the problem, and in 1912 Polish chemist Casimir Funk discovered that by giving his pigeons the hulls that had been removed from the rice grain, the pigeons recovered from the disease.

Funk dubbed the magical ingredient in the hulls "vitamine," from the Latin *vita* meaning "life," and *amine* meaning "nitrogen-containing compound." Within four years, Elmer McCullum, a famed nutritionist in Wisconsin, studied vitamine further and found it didn't contain nitrogen but two other substances: vitamin B and vitamin A (as he called them).

During the 1920s, McCullum's work with vitamins became known as the Newer Nutrition. Soon, new vitamin substances found in citrus fruits captured America's imagination. But the nation wasn't really concerned with vitamin deficiency diseases such as beriberi and scurvy. "Rather, what struck home were indications that the newly discovered substances affected health, longevity and growth," writes Harvey Levenstein, author of *Revolution at the Table*. Dietary supplements rapidly grew in popularity during the 1930s and 40s. Because many processed foods lack nutrients, manufacturers began fortifying these foods with vitamins at this time. By 1945, vitamins and other supplements ranked among the most popular products in health food stores.

HEALTH REASONS TO TAKE DIETARY SUPPLEMENTS

Scientists have identified 13 organic substances commonly labeled vitamins. These play a key role in maintaining good health, including helping the body regulate chemical reactions that protect cells from the effects of aging and environmental pollution as well as converting food into energy and living tissue.

There was a time when vitamins were primarily thought of as substances to prevent nutritional deficiency diseases. That's the reasoning behind the creation of the Recommended Dietary Allowances (RDAs) found on the backs of cereal boxes and other food labels, says nutrition expert Jeffrey S. Bland, Ph.D. U.S. health officials believed that if they identified the amount of a nutrient needed to prevent a deficiency disease then increased this amount slightly, this standard would represent the intake of a specific vitamin required to meet the needs of practically all healthy people. True enough, but Bland and other experts point out that RDAs probably aren't meaningful when it comes to achieving optimal health. For instance, supplements might be essential for anyone with special nutritional needs — anyone who's wounded or burned, has recently undergone surgery, suffers from intestinal malabsorption, is overweight, uses prescription drugs that block the effects of certain vitamins, consumes alcohol, is pregnant, or is of a unique genetic makeup that requires higher intakes for normal function.

This thought frames vitamins in a new light. Vitamin A, for example, prevents the deficiency disease xerophthalmia, a common cause of blindness among malnourished children. However, researchers believe vitamin A might also reduce the risk of heart disease, stroke, and breast, lung, colon, prostate and cervical cancers. And the list goes on. Many scientists now believe all antioxidants — including vitamins A, C and E and the minerals selenium, zinc, copper and manganese — may help prevent cancer, joint inflammation and other diseases. Chromium may help reduce blood cholesterol levels. Zinc may ease prostate problems and improve sexual function in men. In fact, many diseases suffered by the elderly may be the result of a lifetime of suboptimal nutrition, which contributes to wear and tear on the body and ultimately leads to disease, Edward Schneider, M.D., former director of the National Institute on Aging, writes in the *New England Journal of Medicine*. He suggests the United States adopt vitamin standards for optimal health, not just adequate intakes for the prevention of deficiency diseases.

U.S. health officials are considering revising the RDAs by the mid-1990s to reflect recent scientific advances in vitamin use. However, many Americans, relying on both emerging science and their own common sense, aren't waiting for new standards to be released. Pollsters estimate 90 million Americans regularly use vitamins, spending nearly $5 billion a year on them.

Supplement Quality Varies Widely

Dietary supplements aren't created equal. Many supplements, over-the-counter medicines and diet aids carried by natural products retailers are better formulated than the inexpensive, commercially prepared products available at supermarkets, according to Peter Dakin, C.N., author of *Dakin's Reference and Product Guide*.

Dakin's book describes the ingredients in more than 100 products, noting what's missing in addition to what's included. For example, one commercially popular brand of children's vitamins includes no minerals. Another uses the artificial sweetener aspartame. One best-selling adult multivitamin contains synthetic vitamin E, sugar, sodium, and artificial preservatives and coloring.

Although in some cases there may be little or no difference between commercial and natural supplements, experts say it pays to read labels and do a little research. The vitamins and minerals sold in natural products stores tend to avoid artificial ingredients and questionable fillers. Vitamin E is available from natural sources, for instance, and it's also an effective natural preservative conscientious manufacturers use in place of artificial preservatives. Supplements sold by natural products retailers are also often formulated using the latest nutritional research, meaning they may have the best dissolution and absorption rates, use the highest quality ingredients, or target specific nutritional needs rather than take a "shotgun" approach to supplementation.

Many natural products retailers own a copy of Dakin's guide and would be happy to share it with you.

ECONOMICAL REASONS TO BUY SUPPLEMENTS

Simply put, the cost of preventing disease is much less than the cost of treating disease. The research clearly shows that antioxidants such as vitamins A, C, E and selenium can prevent cancer and heart disease and slow the aging process. "For example, there is extensive evidence," says Rob McCaleb, president of the Herb Research Foundation in Boulder, Colo., "that a few pennies of vitamin E taken everyday can prevent or delay a heart attack. In fact, 80 percent of physicians are convinced this is true and are using this procedure today."

This is especially true for cancer prevention, notes McCaleb. "In the majority of cases, cancer treatment is highly expensive and ineffective. It's the task of our immune systems to destroy abnormal cells thus preventing clusters of abnormal cells from turning into tumors. That makes a strong case for immune stimulants and antioxidants, which destroy free radicals that damage DNA and cause malignancies."

Nutrients To Help You Fight Illness

Certain vitamins and minerals aid your body's immune system and can help you fight off colds, flus and other illnesses. Here's a quick guide to some of the best:

NUTRIENT:	BENEFIT:
Beta-Carotene (Precursor to vitamin A)	May help boost activity of white blood cells that detoxify your system. May strengthen membranes to resist penetration of allergens and protect against or alleviate an allergic attack. **U.S. RDA:** 5,000 IU
Vitamin B-3 (Niacin)	An essential part of immune system function. May help lower cholesterol. **U.S. RDA:** 20 mg.
Vitamin B-6 (Pyridoxine)	Used to manufacture adrenal hormones that make antibodies to knock out allergens. **U.S. RDA:** 2 mg.
Vitamin C	May detoxify foreign substances penetrating the immune system. May keep cell walls and connective tissue strong to repel allergens. May stimulate lymphocytes to react faster to germs. **U.S. RDA:** 60 mg.
Vitamin E	Deficiency may be associated with depressed immune system responses. May be an immune system stimulant. **U.S. RDA:** 8-10 IU
Selenium	Retards aging. Works synergistically with vitamin E to make vitamin E more effective. **U.S. RDA:** 70 mcg. (men), 55 mcg. (women)
Zinc	Essential for effective immune response against bacteria and viruses. Cell growth and white blood cell reproduction is dependent on zinc. There also may be a connection between zinc deficiency and destruction of immune memory cells, which store immunization information. **U.S. RDA:** 15 mg.

Sources: *Immune Power Boosters* (Prentice Hall) by Carlson Wade; *Complete Book of Vitamins and Minerals for Health* (Rodale Press); *Fighting Disease: Complete Guide to Natural Immune Power* (Rodale Press); *The Immune System* (Keats) by Neil Orenstein; and Earl Mindell, R.Ph., Ph.D.

How to Choose Supplements

When you take nutritional supplements, you might assume you're getting the full benefit of the nutrition they contain. But that's rarely the case, warns Bland.

Some nutrients block absorption of others, and some food ingredients interfere with the absorption of certain nutrients. For instance, Bland says women who take high levels of calcium risk magnesium deficiencies because the two minerals are interdependent and must be balanced to be properly absorbed by the body. Similarly, supplementing with high doses of iron can result in insufficiencies of manganese and calcium. In addition, some supplements don't break down easily in the digestive tract and aren't completely absorbed. When it comes to supplements, it's important to remember that we aren't "what we eat," but rather "what we absorb from what we eat," Bland says.

Here's a quick guide to maximizing the effectiveness of the supplements you take:

MULTIVITAMINS
Check their dissolve rate. A capsule or tablet should dissolve in vinegar in one hour.

VITAMIN A
Take with vitamins D and E as well as selenium to increase potency.

VITAMIN B
Take as B-complex because the B vitamins have a synergistic effect when they're taken together.

VITAMIN C
Take with a meal. Balance with vitamin E for the most benefit. Use the buffered form (calcium ascorbate, sodium ascorbate) if you have digestive problems.

FAT-SOLUBLE VITAMINS (A, D, E, CAROTENE)
Absorption is enhanced if taken at a meal which includes fat.

VITAMIN E
Inorganic iron (ferrous sulphate) destroys vitamin E. Take only with organic iron (ferrous gluconate, ferrous fumarate) if you also take iron.

MINERALS
Use chelated forms.

CALCIUM
Take with milk. Balance calcium with magnesium by taking twice as much calcium as magnesium daily. Take calcium citrate for optimal absorption.

IRON
Absorption is enhanced by vitamin C. Balance with manganese and calcium. Take iron fumarate to avoid gastrointestinal upset.

MAGNESIUM
Take separately from meals because it neutralizes stomach acid.

SELENIUM
Take as selenomethionine. Balance with vitamin E to achieve synergistic effects.

Designing Your Supplement Program

Because everyone's nutritional needs vary widely, it's impossible to say exactly what and how many supplements a particular individual's diet should include. However, the following chart provides some general guidelines to the uses of common vitamins and minerals for the average adult. (This chart is not meant to replace the advice of a health care practitioner):

VITAMIN A (BETA-CAROTENE)
- **RDA:** 5,000 IU
- **Principal Functions:** Maintains skin, mucous membranes. Increases resistance to infection. Promotes healthy eye tissue and enhances night vision.
- **Deficiency Symptoms:** Night blindness; abnormal eye dryness; rough, itchy skin; susceptibility to respiratory infection.
- **Latest Research:** May lower risk of cardiovascular disease and lung, stomach and mouth cancers. May increase children's resistance to infection.

THIAMINE (VITAMIN B-1)
- **RDA:** 1.5 mg.
- **Principal Functions:** Promotes carbohydrate utilization for energy. Aids nervous system function.
- **Deficiency Symptoms:** Confusion; fatigue; insomnia; irritability; eye muscle weakness; loss of appetite, memory, concentration.
- **Latest Research:** There may be a link between thiamine deficiency and anorexia, depression, neurological complications. May help wounds heal.

RIBOFLAVIN (VITAMIN B-2)
- **RDA:** 1.7 mg.
- **Principal Functions:** Aids production, utilization of energy in body cells. Promotes healthy skin, eyes.
- **Deficiency Symptoms:** Anemia; discolored tongue; scaly skin; burning, itchy red eyes.
- **Latest Research:** Deficiency may cause decreased ability to make illness-fighting antibodies.

NIACIN (VITAMIN B-3)
- **RDA:** 20 mg.
- **Principal Functions:** Aids fat synthesis, tissue respiration, carbohydrate utilization. Promotes healthy skin, nerves and digestive tract. Aids digestive system.
- **Deficiency Symptoms:** Dermatitis; insomnia; mental depression; headache; diarrhea; gum and tongue ulceration.
- **Latest Research:** Possible cancer inhibitor. May lower cholesterol. Essential to immune system function.

PYRIDOXINE (VITAMIN B-6)
- **RDA:** 2 mg.
- **Principal Functions:** Assists in red blood cell regeneration. Helps regulate protein, fat and carbohydrate use.
- **Deficiency Symptoms:** Depression; nervousness; lethargy; water retention; appetite loss; diarrhea.
- **Latest Research:** May enhance immunity in the elderly. Prevents neural tube defects in fetuses. May help control premenstrual depression.

FOLIC ACID (VITAMIN B-9)
- **RDA:** 200 mcg.
- **Principal Functions:** Aids normal blood formation. Helps enzyme and other biochemical systems function.
- **Deficiency Symptoms:** Anemia; intestinal complaints; dizziness; fatigue; shortness of breath.
- **Latest Research:** Is necessary for healthy development of fetuses.

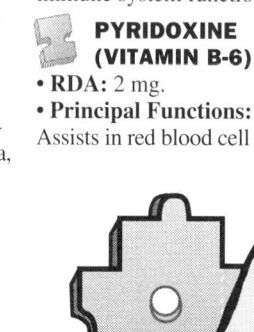

Illustration by Debra Page-Trim

Supplements

PANTOTHENIC ACID
- **RDA:** 7 mg.
- **Principal Functions:** Protects against anemia.
- **Deficiency Symptoms:** N/A
- **Latest Research:** N/A

VITAMIN C
- **RDA:** 60 mg.
- **Principal Functions:** Forms substances such as collagen that hold body cells together. Strengthens blood vessels, hastens healing, increases infection resistance and aids iron utilization.
- **Deficiency Symptoms:** Easy bruising; bleeding, receding gums and dental problems; slow healing; fatigue; rough skin.
- **Latest Research:** May reduce risk of heart disease (in part by cutting cholesterol), cancers of the mouth, esophagus and stomach. May protect lungs against pollutants. May naturally combat cold, allergies.

VITAMIN D
- **RDA:** 400 IU
- **Principal Functions:** Transports calcium. Promotes intestinal and renal absorption phosphate.
- **Deficiency Symptoms:** N/A
- **Latest Research:** May help prevent osteoporosis and kidney disease.

VITAMIN E
- **RDA:** 8-10 IU
- **Principal Functions:** Antioxidant that protects vitamin A and unsaturated fatty acids from destruction by oxygen. May also help maintain cell membrane integrity.
- **Deficiency Symptoms:** Muscle degeneration; anemia; nerve dysfunction; skin pigmentation.
- **Latest Research:** May lower risk of cardiovascular disease, cancers and cataracts. May enhance immune response.

CALCIUM
- **RDA:** 1,000 mg.
- **Principal Functions:** Used in formation of bones and teeth. Aids in blood clotting, cell membrane permeability, neuromuscular activity.
- **Deficiency Symptoms:** Osteoporosis.
- **Latest Research:** May enhance the rate of increase in bone mineral density in children and help prevent osteoporosis.

IRON
- **RDA:** 15 mg.
- **Principal Functions:** Constituent of hemoglobin, myoglobin, catalase, cytochromes. Enzyme cofactor.
- **Deficiency Symptoms:** Anemia marked by chronic fatigue and weakness.
- **Latest Research:** Deficiency linked to anemia. May cause an increase in attentiveness.

MAGNESIUM
- **RDA:** 400 mg.
- **Principal Functions:** Constituent of bones and teeth. Decreases neuromuscular sensitivity. Enzyme cofactor.
- **Deficiency Symptoms:** Weakness; muscle tremors; anorexia.
- **Latest Research:** May help prevent cancers, osteoporosis, cardiovascular disease. May reduce cholesterol.

ZINC
- **RDA:** 15 mg.
- **Principal Functions:** Constituent of insulin, carbonic anhydrase and other enzymes. Essential for cell growth and production of disease-fighting white blood cells.
- **Deficiency Symptoms:** N/A
- **Latest Research:** May have role in maintaining healthy brain tissue. May prevent certain types of neurological disease. May prevent prostate problems and increase fertility. May help prevent certain cancers.

Don't Forget Beneficial Bacteria

Almost everyone knows that vitamins and minerals are important. But you shouldn't overlook another type of dietary supplement: beneficial bacteria.

The human body is home to tens of millions of bacterial organisms that are essential to good health, says herbalist and medical botanist Christopher Hobbs. For instance, beneficial bacteria in the intestines help digest foods, create vitamins and inhibit the growth of disease-promoting pathogenic bacteria. Some beneficial microorganisms have been shown to produce natural antibiotics, anticarcinogens, anticholesteremic substances and compounds that break down and recycle toxins.

Many people have traditionally eaten certain cultured and fermented foods rich in beneficial bacteria, including yogurt and sauerkraut. Today, however, a variety of supplements rich in beneficial bacteria such as acidophilus and lactobacillus also are available as powders, capsules, tablets and liquids.

When should you consider taking beneficial bacteria? Hobbs recommends using them during:

- **ANTIBIOTIC TREATMENTS** — such treatments can strip the digestive tract of beneficial bacteria.

- **CONSTIPATION** — long-term use of beneficial bacteria can promote regularity.

- **PREGNANCY** — beneficial bacteria can promote regular bowel movements and may aid breastfeeding.

- **INFECTIONS** — beneficial bacteria may help fight urinary tract, bowel, gum and tooth, and vaginal infections.

Supplementing children's diets with bifidobacteria may also support immunity, establish a strong probiotic flora in their growing intestinal tracts and protect against diarrhea and other bowel disorders, Hobbs says.

One warning: You might produce abnormal amounts of gas after beginning a probiotic supplementation program. The condition will normalize, and you can ease into the program by taking half the recommended amount for a week or two.

❝ It's time to change the focus of the RDA from the 1940s to the 21st century. A growing wave of scientific research shows optimal intakes of certain nutrients can reduce the risk of cancer, heart disease, osteoporosis, birth defects and other medical conditions. ❞

— *J.B. Cordero, president of the Council for Responsible Nutrition, which represents the supplement industry*

Essential Nutrients for Men and Women

Because of their biological differences, men and women have unique nutritional needs. Here are some vitamins and minerals of particular importance to each of the sexes:

Women

NUTRIENT: Calcium
PROPERTIES: Prevents osteoporosis, which is primarily a women's disease. Also alleviates premenstrual stress, cramps and water retention.

NUTRIENT: Folic acid (vitamin B-9)
PROPERTIES: Essential for fetal development. Prevents birth defects such as spina bifida and anencephaly. Also alleviates heavy menstrual bleeding and hemorrhaging in childbirth. Improves lactation.

NUTRIENT: Iron
PROPERTIES: Necessary for production of hemoglobin, the oxygen-carrying component of red blood cells. Women with heavy menstrual flows often have iron-deficiency anemia.

NUTRIENT: Manganese
PROPERTIES: A component of female sex hormones; necessary for normal reproduction. Essential for milk production, therefore pregnant or lactating women need increased amounts. Also helpful in preventing osteoporosis.

NUTRIENT: Pyridoxine (vitamin B-6)
PROPERTIES: Women using oral contraceptives need increased amounts of vitamin B-6 to prevent phlebitis. Essential during pregnancy to relieve morning sickness and prevent toxemia and leg cramps. Also eases premenstrual anxiety (including depression) and reduces water retention.

Men

NUTRIENT: Beta-carotene (vitamin A precursor)
PROPERTIES: Essential for health of male reproductive organs. Needed for sperm production.

NUTRIENT: Magnesium
PROPERTIES: Necessary for testosterone production. Helpful in correcting prostate problems and sterility.

NUTRIENT: Selenium
PROPERTIES: Essential for sperm production. In combination with vitamin E and zinc, selenium provides relief from enlarged prostate gland.

NUTRIENT: Zinc
PROPERTIES: Important in the development of male reproductive organs; necessary for testosterone production. Aids in the treatment of infertility and prevents prostate problems. Boosts sex drive.

Sources: *The Natural Remedy Book for Women* (Crossing Press) by Diane Stein; *The Male Herbal: Health Care for Men & Boys* (Crossing Press) by James Green; and *Prescription for Nutritional Healing* (Avery Publishing) by James Balch, M.D., and Phyllis Balch, C.N.C.

Chapter 2
HERBS

*How To Buy
Herbs, Homeopathy and Aromatherapy*

Herbal medicine is believed to be one of the world's oldest healing models. Medicinal herbs have been found near Stone Age sites. In China, herbalism's roots are thought to spread as far back as 5,400 years to Shen Nung, who according to Chinese legend was responsible for the development of modern agriculture, animal domestication and discovery of the therapeutic value of herbs. In addition, written records of medical herb use by the Egyptians date to 2000 B.C. In the West, Native Americans have practiced herbalism for centuries.

Although herbal medicine is growing in the United States, it's studied and practiced more commonly elsewhere. In France and Germany, for instance, *Ginkgo Biloba*, a natural extract from the leaf of an ancient tree that stimulates blood flow to the limbs and brain, is frequently used to increase cognitive function and memory.

ECONOMICAL REASONS TO BUY HERBS

Today, more and more researchers are finding that herbal medicines are often safer, less expensive and at least as effective as other drugs, according to the Herb Research Foundation, a nonprofit educational and scientific organization in Boulder, Colo. For example, clinical studies show that simple garlic can reduce blood cholesterol and blood pressure, two contributors to heart disease, with no side effects and at a cost of pennies a day. In addition, an extract of licorice root has been shown to safely and effectively heal ulcers of the small intestines at a cost of $10 to $20 a month. This compares favorably to use of Tagamet®, a cimetidine-containing drug, which costs nearly $70 for a one-month supply and may induce side effects including confusion, drowsiness, irregular heart beat and impotency.

ENVIRONMENTAL REASONS TO BUY HERBS

Besides being safe and effective, herbs are also environmentally friendly. Conscientious herbalists conserve the wild plants their trade depends upon. Concerned that some plants are being overharvested as public demand for them grows, many herbalists encourage a system of wildcrafting that actually promotes species survival. (Wildcrafters collect herbs from the wild rather than from cultivated gardens). "A good wildcrafter should be able to increase the population of plants instead of decrease it. It's just like pruning — wildcrafting actually encourages proliferation, and for our good deed, we get to take some home," herbalist Ed Smith from Oregon says. In some cases, wildcrafting not only protects the herbalist's trade and safeguards valuable resources, but also provides a renewable source of income for local workers. Taking herbs, nuts and other renewable resources from the rain forests, for instance, can yield far more in the long term than burning the forests down for farmland or cutting them down for lumber.

Plants that are threatened with extinction, as in the case of the wild orchid ladyslipper, are protected by trade organizations overseeing the industry, and herbalists also are cultivating more and more plants that were formerly taken from the wild. Wild American ginseng, for example, has been overharvested in the wild but is now grown on farms. And because these herbs are used to make natural remedies, many of them are organically grown and produced using little or no synthetic pesticides, fertilizers or other farm chemicals.

HEALTH REASONS TO BUY HERBS

"Antibiotics have been seriously overused and we're all paying the price," says Rob McCaleb. "Most physicians know this and most physicians will admit they'll prescribe an antibiotic for a viral condition even though antibiotics aren't effective against viral conditions. They do this to satisfy the patient who expects a prescription. Yet these antibiotics are ineffective and expensive. For example, most physicians know that the herb echinacea is more effective than antibiotics for treating bronchitis in children and that antibiotics will interfere with recovery."

Antibiotic overuse has created new antibiotic-resistant strains that are very difficult to treat such as antibiotic-resistant strep and gonorrhea. "For example, garlic and goldenseal are both highly effective in killing strep," says McCaleb. "And the immune-boosting herbs such as echinacea boost our immune systems to fight the infection. In fact, goldenseal is such a powerful antibiotic that overuse of it can lead to reduced levels of beneficial bacteria in the intestine. Yet, a physician isn't likely to tell us to take goldenseal. He or she will most likely write a prescription for a very costly and ineffective antibiotic."

A Quick Guide to Herbal Preparations

Herbal medicines come in a variety of forms, each with unique benefits. Here's a quick guide to the most common forms:

WHOLE HERBS
Must be cut and sifted or powdered for use in teas or capsules; retain potency for up to two years.

SLICED HERBS (ROOTS & BARKS)
Easier to powder and convenient for making teas; they preserve moderately well.

POWDERED HERBS
Ready to use in capsules or teas; have a shelf life of about one year.

LIQUID EXTRACTS/TINCTURES
Concentrated, the most quickly and efficiently absorbed of any preparation. Herbs can be extracted fresh in the optimum season and their freshness preserved for two to three years; they can be disguised in juice or water for children. There are no standards for liquid formulas in the United States, but historically, extracts are stronger tinctures. Tinctures are defined as alcohol-based extracts.

POWDERED EXTRACTS
Concentrated, efficiently absorbed; taste disguised in capsules or tablets; no alcohol; freshness preserved two to three years.

STANDARDIZED POWDERED EXTRACTS
All the advantages of powdered extracts, but active constituents are identified at set levels; herb's original balance might be altered.

OILS, SALVES, CREAMS, OINTMENTS
Herbal extracts in an oil and beeswax or water-soluble base; excellent for external trauma, burns, bites, stings, cuts, aches and pains; easy to carry, convenient.

SYRUPS, ELIXIRS
Herbal extracts in a sweet base; sweet tasting, palatable for children (and adults sensitive to strong tastes); can coat and soothe the throat to help relieve coughs; concentrated; fast acting.

LOZENGES
Herbal extracts in a candy base; sweet tasting, palatable for children of all ages; convenient to carry and use for sore throats and upper-respiratory imbalance.

Milk Thistle

Common Herbs and Their Uses

This chart is not intended to replace the advice of a physician.

Herbs for Stress

ASTRAGALUS
Indications: Low energy; lethargy.
Benefits: Supports immune function, especially against cancer, AIDS and other deficiency diseases.

GINSENG
Indications: General weakness, especially involving digestion.
Benefits: General adaptogen.

GOTU KOLA
Indications: Weak memory, brain function; poorly healing external wounds; eruptive skin disease; diarrhea.
Benefits: Stimulates healing and regeneration.

HO-SHOU-WU
Indications: Prematurely white hair; weak kidneys and liver; sexual disinterest; loose bowels; constipation; coronary heart disease.
Benefits: Increases vigor and regularity.

LICORICE
Indications: Adrenal weakness; ulcers; viral infection; general weakness; throat dryness; cough; toxicity.
Benefits: Stimulates the adrenal glands and promotes vitality.

SCHIZANDRA
Indications: Low mental energy; liver illness; toxicity.
Benefits: Strengthens lungs and kidneys; supports digestion.

SIBERIAN GINSENG
Indications: General stress; life changes; travel; blood sugar swings.
Benefits: Increases work performance; prevents illness.

SUMA
Indications: Premenstrual syndrome; moodiness; blood sugar swings.
Benefits: Protects against cancer; balances sugar metabolism; protects against PMS, hormone imbalance; supports vital energy.

Herbs for Immunity

ASTRAGALUS
Indications: Colds; flus; viral infections.
Benefits: Stimulates white blood cell activity.

ECHINACEA
Indications: Colds; flus; viral infections; hay fever.
Benefits: Mobilizes white blood cells; disintegrates bacteria; kills viruses; helps protect cells from infection.

GOLDENSEAL
Indications: Colds; flus; viral infections; hay fever; upper respiratory or urinary tract infections; inflammation; ulcers (and general problems with mucous membranes such as pinkeye); mild bowel irritations.
Benefits: Antifungal and antibacterial; improves circulation; anti-inflammatory; improves digestion,

(Common Herbs and Their Uses Cont.)

increasing production of digestive enzymes and hydrochloric acid; cleansing; liver tonic.

SHIITAKE MUSHROOM
Indications: Tumors; cancer; leukemia; lymphosarcoma; Hodgkin's Disease; flus; viral infections.
Benefits: Reverses T-cell suppression caused by tumors; inhibits viral cell division; anti-inflammatory.

Herbs for Relaxation & Sleep

CHAMOMILE
Indications: Tense or cramped muscles.
Benefits: Muscle relaxant.

HOPS
Indications: Muscle tension; nervousness; insomnia.
Benefits: Reduces muscle tension; calms the nerves; mild sedative.

PASSION FLOWER
Indications: Insomnia; nervousness.
Benefits: Calms the nerves.

ST. JOHN'S WORT
Indications: Depression; insomnia.
Benefits: Boosts the spirits; mild sedative.

VALERIAN
Indications: Insomnia; nervousness; tension; anxiety.
Benefits: Mild sedative; soothes nerves and eases muscle tension.

Herbs for Sports

AMERICAN GINSENG
Function: Adaptogen.
Benefits: Helps body adapt to physical stress; enhances energy.

CHINESE ASTRAGALUS
Function: Energy tonic.
Benefits: Strengthens body energy; enhances resistance; tones the lungs.

SIBERIAN GINSENG
Function: Adaptogen.
Benefits: Helps body adapt to physical stress; enhances recovery and endurance.

Herbs for Women's Health

(If pregnant, consult your doctor before taking herbs)

CHASTE BERRY
Indications: Low or high sex drive; irregular menstruation; PMS; nursing.
Benefits: Normalizes sex drive; eases depression; alleviates migraine headaches; premenstrual acne; breast tenderness; cramps and bloating; regulates ovulation; increases milk flow.

DONG QUAI
Indications: PMS; menstrual cramps; hot flashes; absence of menstruation.
Benefits: Helps alleviate hot flashes and vaginal atrophy (characterized by decreased lubrication and thinning of vaginal membranes); eases PMS-oriented depression; improves circulation; relaxing; tonifying; may help prepare the uterus for conception.

RASPBERRY LEAF
Indications: Pregnancy; menstruation; menopause.
Benefits: Generally strengthens and tones the reproductive system; eases cramps and prepares the uterus for childbirth.

SIBERIAN GINSENG
Indications: Stress; fatigue; illness.
Benefits: A tonic with adaptogenic qualities; tones and balances bodily functions; boosts energy and immunity.

Herbs for Asthma & Allergies

EYEBRIGHT
Indications: Burning eyes; inflamed nasal passages.
Benefits: Anti-inflammatory.

EPHEDRA
Indications: Congestion.
Benefits: Decongestant; reduces allergic reactions.

NETTLES
Indications: Fever; runny itchy eyes; congestion.
Benefits: Blood purifier; kidney stimulator; rich in vitamin C and chlorophyll.

The Art of Aromatherapy

Aromatherapy, the art of using pure aromatic essential plant oils to enhance health and well-being, is becoming more and more popular. In many cases, the oils are placed in a diffuser, and the scent affects the brain through the olfactory nerves, resulting in conditions such as tranquility or stimulation of the circulatory system. In other cases, the oils are diluted in a carrier oil such as jojoba and applied to the skin. (Consult a health care practitioner before applying an undiluted essential oil directly to the skin as some oils may cause irritation.) In either case, aromatherapy can be a simple, potent and nonintrusive means of healing. Here are some botanical scents and their properties from the *Aromatherapy Workbook* by Marcel Lavabre:

BERGAMOT Antiseptic for acne; balances nervous system; uplifting; avoid using before sunning, as it increases sun sensitivity.

CHAMOMILE Soothes inflamed skin; headache; insomnia; toothache; balances female reproductive system; calms anger.

CLARY SAGE Regenerates skin; soothes inflamed skin; balances female reproductive system; calms stress and relieves depression.

EUCALYPTUS Balances energy; respiratory system antiseptic; expectorant for asthma and bronchitis.

JASMINE Soothes dry skin; relieves anxiety, lethargy and depression; aphrodisiac.

LAVENDER Soothes acne and oily skin; antiseptic for burns, abscesses and wounds; decongestant; antidepressant; calming.

PEPPERMINT Skin cleanser; stimulates metabolism, nervous system; eases dyspepsia, nausea and vomiting; soothes fever; relieves muscular pain; helps depression and mental strain.

ROSE Regenerates skin cells and moisturizes dry skin; aphrodisiac; regulates female reproductive system; emotionally uplifting; soothes shock and grief.

ROSEMARY Acne antiseptic; rejuvenates aged skin; regulates dandruff and oily hair; uplifting; relieves mental strain.

SANDALWOOD Elevates emotions; grounding; antidepressant.

SPEARMINT Digestive aid; soothes depression and mental fatigue.

TEA TREE For skin irritations, acne and dandruff; antiseptic for respiratory system, urinary infections; soothes athlete's foot, candida, fungal infections, ringworm and vaginitis; helps infected wounds.

YLANG YLANG Soothes hypertension; aphrodisiac; calms anger, fear and nervous tension.

Homeopathic Medicine: An Alternative

Homeopathic doctors look at medicine differently than conventional doctors. Rather than stifle physical problems with high doses of drugs, homeopaths employ a holistic approach to healing that includes the use of more than 2,000 plant- and mineral-based medicines. These highly diluted medicines result in few, if any, side effects and are designed to stimulate the body's own healing mechanisms — a time-tested approach described as "the Law of Similars," or "like cures like." The practice maintains that substances which produce certain disease symptoms in a healthy person can be used to treat the same symptoms in a sick patient. Approved by the Food and Drug Administration, many of these natural medicines have been used in the United States since the turn of the century and are available at natural products stores. Some homeopathic remedies are easily neutralized by external substances such as mint in toothpaste. Therefore, the mouth environment should be free of chemicals before you take these remedies. Here's a quick reference guide to some common ailments and their homeopathic remedies:

> **THE DOCTOR AMUSES THE PATIENT WHILE NATURE CURES THE ILLNESS.**
> —*VOLTAIRE*

AILMENT:	REMEDY:
Colds	Allium cepa
Bee sting	Apis mellifica
Injury	Arnica montana
Diarrhea	Arsenicum album
Fever	Belladonna
Arthritis	Bryonia
Cough	Bryonia
Bladder infections	Cantharis
Colic	Chamomilla
Anxiety/grief	Ignatia
PMS/hot flashes	Lachesis
Cramps	Magnesium phosphoricum
Headache/hangover	Nux vomica
Asthma/allergies/ear infections	Pulsatilla
Joint pain/stiffness	Rhus toxicodendron
Eczema	Sepia
Skin rash	Sulphur

How to Create a Natural First Aid Kit

Herbs have been used for first aid for thousands of years, says Feather Jones, an herbalist and founding member of the Rocky Mountain Herbalist Coalition. Herbs can boost the immune system, alleviate toxic conditions and support and stimulate the healing process.

Jones says the basics of any first aid kit include scissors, tweezers, mirror, thermometer, gauze, cloth tape, sterile pads, bandages, butterfly-type bandages, CPR and choking instructions and an Ace bandage. However, she adds, natural herbal medicines make welcome additions. Here's a guide to some common first aid medicines that you can make yourself or buy pre-prepared:

Herbal Extracts

ARNICA This external remedy makes a great massage liniment for sore and cramped muscles. It decreases pain, swelling and bruising. It works best if applied immediately after an injury and continued every couple of hours for the first day.

CAYENNE Used internally for frostbite and hypothermia, cayenne moves the blood from the center of the body to the peripheral areas. It can help revive someone in shock or trauma. Used externally, it helps coagulate blood to stop bleeding.

ECHINACEA In addition to its ability to boost immune function by increasing white blood cells in an infected area when taken internally, echinacea is antibiotic and antibacterial to bacteria such as strep and staph. It's helpful with fevers, poisoning or any type of internal infection.

GRINDELIA Used externally, grindelia cools and soothes hot, irritated skin, rashes, sunburns and insect bites. Internally, it helps expel mucus in the bronchial passages and may be useful for some cases of asthma and respiratory congestion.

SYRUP OF IPECAC Ipecac taken internally promotes vomiting. It should be used only for certain types of poisoning.

VALERIAN OR POPPY As an antispasmodic (taken internally) and painkiller, these two herbs relieve intestinal cramps, headaches and general aches or pains. As nervines, they help induce sleep.

FLOWER REMEDIES Used for emotional trauma, these remedies work quickly and effectively on symptoms ranging from hyperventilation to hysteria.

Powdered Herbs

GINGERROOT A couple of capsules help prevent motion and morning sickness as well as nausea due to flu or bad food.

POULTICE POWDER This should consist of at least one antifungal herb, one antibacterial herb, an emollient and an astringent. For example: gentian, myrrh gum, propolis and comfrey root. Great for sore feet, lacerations, diaper rash, infections, insect bites or inflamed eyes (when mixed into a tea and used as a wash).

SLIPPERY ELM Slippery elm capsules buffer poisons in the stomach and bowels to decrease toxic absorption. The herb also can soothe mucous membranes and settle an upset stomach.

Oils

PEPPERMINT Add a little oil of peppermint to water and take internally to help settle an upset stomach or rub a little on the temples to stay awake.

TEA TREE Called the "first aid kit in a bottle," tea tree contains strong antifungal and antibiotic properties with antiseptic properties. It can be used externally for earaches, fungal infections, pus-filled wounds or burns, cold sores and herpes lesions. It also makes an excellent insect repellant.

Salves

CALENDULA This herb is famous for its antibacterial properties. It speeds healing and minimizes scar tissue.

COMFREY Used externally it stimulates cell growth and tissue repair. The allantoin in comfrey is soothing. Don't take comfrey internally.

Gingerroot

Chapter 3
PERSONAL CARE

How To Buy Personal Care Products

HEALTH REASONS TO USE NATURAL COSMETICS

Next time you shop for organic and whole foods at your neighborhood natural products store, take a look at the new face they're putting on their personal care products area. You'll find non-toxic, natural, biodegradable products that rival mass market or salon products in performance and price. Use your buying power to let retailers know you care enough to be committed to Earthwise, quality natural ingredients. Your commitment to demand safer, high-quality personal care products can create momentum for another healthy change in the world.

Instead of using pore-clogging mineral oil, for instance, try natural skin lotions which contain jojoba, sunflower or borage oils that are lighter and provide the skin with nutrients. Another example is the industry's use of natural pigments rather than synthetic dyes. Although natural pigments don't offer the variety of vivid colors that can be produced synthetically, they also aren't saddled with a history of carcinogenicity and allergic reactions caused by FD&C dyes. One recent study found that women who use synthetic hair dyes had a 50 percent greater chance of developing non-Hodgkin's lymphoma than women who had never dyed their hair. Synthetic dyes also can damage the hair and may cause nausea, hives, scalp irritation and facial swelling.

In fact, many synthetic ingredients raise health concerns because they can actually harm the skin more than they help it and also may contribute to debilitating environmental sensitivities or other illnesses. For example, researchers recently found that multiple myeloma, a malignant tumor of the bone marrow, occurred at four times the rate of the general population in the

58,000 hairdressers, manicurists and cosmetologists they studied. Effects ranging from skin irritations to chromosomal damage have been traced to repeated use of synthetic ingredients found in personal care products. Ingredients to watch for — and avoid — include mineral oil, petrolatum, isopropyl myristate, artificial fragrances, triethanolamine, phenol (carbolic acid), propylene glycol and sodium lauryl sulfate.

Shoppers for natural cosmetics need to do a little homework, however, if they want to make informed buying decisions, warns Zia Wesley-Hosford, author of six books on skin care and cosmetics and publisher of the newsletter *Great Face*. Some beneficial natural moisturizing ingredients such as hyaluronic acid and sodium PCA have chemical or unnatural sounding names that make it difficult to distinguish the good from the bad, she says. Titanium dioxide might sound like it would bring Superman to his knees, but it's actually a white pigment formed naturally in three types of crystals that's used in antiperspirants and protective creams. Phenethyl alcohol sounds dangerous, but it's a natural preservative found in oranges, raspberries and teas. Tocopherol is another name for vitamin E; sodium lauryl sulfate is a coconut oil derivative.

Not all natural ingredients are beneficial to the skin, however, Wesley-Hosford says. For instance, coconut oil and cocoa butter are natural, yet they're saturated fats whose molecules are too large for use on facial skin. Moisturizers containing these ingredients can cause pimples, blackheads and skin bumps. Better alternatives include oils of grape seed, avocado, jojoba, rice bran, squalene (from Spanish olives), safflower, sunflower, wheat germ and evening primrose. Oils such as these closely resemble and help replace sebum, the skin's natural moisturizer. As we age, the body's production of sebum slows, making the skin drier. Other helpful natural moisturizers include aloe vera, seaweed and algae extracts, glycerin, lecithin, shea butter and a myriad of botanical extracts.

"The more you learn about both good and bad ingredients in personal care products, the better able you'll be to choose products that work well for your skin," Wesley-Hosford says.

ENVIRONMENTAL REASONS TO USE NATURAL COSMETICS

Natural cosmetics are better for the environment than petroleum-based products, which are made with highly refined chemicals that don't always easily biodegrade. Better yet, natural cosmetics frequently also are cruelty free, which generally means their formulations contain no animal ingredients and that their components haven't been tested on animals for at least three to five years.

Many conventional manufacturers continue to test every ingredient and formulation on animals even though nonanimal tests often are just as effective and cost one-tenth as much, an average of about

> **HEALTH SPAS HAVE LONG RELIED ON THE MAGIC OF WATER — HOT AND COLD — MIXED WITH MUD, HERBS, THE ESSENTIAL PLANT OILS, OR CAREFULLY SELECTED MINERAL SALTS TO SMOOTH SKIN, RELAX TENSE MUSCLES, REFINE PORES AND REVITALIZE BODIES.**
>
> —Leslie Kenton, author of The Joy of Beauty (Doubleday)

$50,000 per product compared to $500,000 for animal testing, according to People for the Ethical Treatment of Animals (PETA) in Washington, D.C. An estimated 14 million animals suffer and die every year in the United States to test the safety of cosmetics and household products.

Most natural manufacturers rely instead on historical safety data, computer models and time-tested ingredients to make their cosmetics. Each company's policy is a little different, however, and consumers should be aware that there are no federal rules governing the use of marketing phrases such as "cruelty free," "no slaughterhouse by-products" or "no animal testing." Cruelty-free manufacturers may conduct laboratory tests on: fertilized chicken eggs, whose membranes can't sense pain yet respond like that of the human eye; cell cultures originally taken from animals or baby boys' circumcised foreskin and grown in the lab; and human volunteers. They may also use ingredients mentioned on the Food and Drug Administration's GRAS (Generally Recognized As Safe) list that haven't been tested on animals for years, or use animal-derived by-products.

Two guides are now available to help consumers take the guesswork out of buying cruelty-free cosmetics: *Shopping Guide for Caring Consumers* is published by PETA, P.O. Box 42516, Washington, D.C. 20015, 301-770-PETA; *Personal Care With Principle* is published by the National Anti-Vivisection Society, 53 W. Jackson Blvd., Suite 1552, Chicago, IL 60604-3795, 312-427-6065.

ECONOMICAL REASONS TO USE NATURAL COSMETICS

Remember that every dollar you spend is a vote for the kind of world you want to live in. The money you spend for natural cosmetics supports cruelty-free practices and the development of the herbal industry rather than the development of the petrochemical industry. "The natural substances used in the natural cosmetics industry are sustainable and support sustainable agriculture," notes Rob McCaleb, president, Herb Research Foundation, Boulder, Colo. "And they're probably better for your skin and hair as well."

We vote with our pocketbooks, explains McCaleb. "The dollars you spend determine how our community grows. If we want our community to grow in the direction of organic and natural then that's what we should buy."

How to choose natural shampoos, conditioners & dyes

❏ Shampoos

Natural shampoos are formulated from three basic ingredients: water, cleansing agents and conditioners.

Water makes one of the best base ingredients because other shampoo residues can coat the hair shaft making the hair limp or difficult to style, whereas water helps rinse away those residues.

Instead of petrochemical cleansing agents, look for natural soaps made with coconut, palm kernel or olive oils (such as mild castile soap). Although these natural cleansers won't create as many suds as synthetic detergents, suds aren't necessary to keep hair clean.

Vegetable proteins can strengthen the hair's natural protein just as well as animal proteins such as collagen, keratin and lanolin, which come from cows and sheep. Natural emollients soften and soothe surface tissues and seal in moisture to keep hair supple. Ingredients such as lecithin and betaine reduce static without the potentially toxic side effects of commonly used synthetic compounds. Other herbs can be added to shampoos to help treat specific problems (see related chart).

❏ Conditioners

Natural conditioners are a must, whether your hair is dry, oily or normal. If your hair has been bleached, colored or permed, a conditioner can help temper the damage done.

Hair consists of layers of protein called keratin. The cell walls of the outermost layer, the cuticle, overlap like roof shingles. In healthy hair, the shingles lie flat, leaving hair supple. In damaged or dry hair, the cuticle shingles are broken and create gaps that make hair porous.

Glycogen-balanced protein conditioners can help fill the gaps and repair damaged hair. Look for conditioners that contain essential fatty acids, amino acids (such as cysteine and methionine), herbs containing silicic acid and amino acids (such as rosemary, sage or horsetail), the milk protein lactalbumin, nettles or glycogen polysaccharide. Also look for moisturizing conditioners containing oils such as lavender, sweet almond, avocado, jojoba and lemon.

❏ Dyes

Natural hair coloring products are made from plants or mineral salts. Although they're temporary and don't match the colors and staying power of synthetic dyes, they're nontoxic and won't damage your hair.

Natural dyes stain the cuticle of the hair and don't lift the cuticle or deposit color into the hair shaft (where it's absorbed by the skin and can be more harmful) like synthetic dyes. Hair can be highlighted but not lightened with natural hair products. These products can also darken hair, covering or softening and camouflaging gray hair.

BENEFITTING FROM SKIN-ENRICHING ENZYMES IN FRUIT & VEGETABLES

Plant enzymes help stimulate the life processes in skin cells, making skin firmer and fresher looking. Many European skin-treatment products are based entirely on the actions of plant enzymes. Raw fruits and vegetables are rich in enzymes, and only a small amount is needed. Many natural personal care products incorporate the following botanicals, or buy them in the organic produce section and use a juicer or blender to puree and add them to your favorite mask or use with a facial sauna:

BOTANICAL:	COMPONENTS:
Almond	Oil, natural sugars, calcium, vitamins A and B-complex
Apple	Copper, calcium, magnesium, iron, vitamin C
Apricot	Minerals, vitamin A, essential oil
Banana	Vitamins A, B, C, E, oils, sugars, iron
Chamomile	Azulene, potassium, phosphorus, lime
Carrot	Vitamins A, B, C, D, E, K, iron, iodine, magnesium, potassium
Comfrey	Allantoin, vitamins A and B-12, tannin
Cucumber	Vitamins A, B, C, natural sugars
Kelp	Vitamins B, C, E, iodine, iron
Lemon	Iron, potassium, tannin, citric acid
Mint	Tannin, essential oil, iron
Peach	Vitamins A, C, natural sugars, essential oil, citric acid
Strawberry	Salicylic acid, lime, iron, sodium, vitamin C, tannin

SKIN TYPE:	PROPERTIES:
Dry skin and older skin	Lubricating, calming
Oily skin, blemished skin	Disinfecting, astringent, antiseptic
All	Promotes cell reproduction
Dry skin and older skin with enlarged pores	Astringent, diuretic
Sensitive, allergic, dry and sunburned skin	Healing, soothing, anti-inflammatory
Sensitive, dehydrated, aging, rashes	Stimulates cell reproduction; moisturizer
Dry skin, acne, inflamed, sunburned skin, blemishes	Soothing and healing, cell proliferant, emollient, moisturizer
All skin, especially normal to oily	Helps bleach freckles, soothing, diuretic, antiwrinkle
Aging skin, cellulite	Stimulates circulation, encourages elimination of wastes and water
Oily skin, skin losing its tone or with uneven pigment such as liver spots	Mild bleach, antiseptic, disinfectant
Oily skin, acne, blemished skin, large pores	Antiseptic, soothing, stimulates circulation
All skin, especially dry	Diuretic, soothing, anti-inflammatory
Oily skin, uneven pigmentation	Astringent, diuretic, toning

Here's a brief guide to natural hair care ingredients from personal care expert Linda Upton, M.Ed., and other authorities:

Healthy Hair Ingredients

ACACIA
Acts as a suspending and emulsifying agent in hair sprays.

ARNICA
Stimulant used in hair tonics.

BETAINE
Conditions; neutralizes negatively charged flyaway hair.

BIRCH
Antiseptic and astringent.

CHAMOMILE
Kills bacteria, neutralizes irritants and strengthens tissues.

CLOVER
An emollient that helps kill bacteria.

GINGER
Mixed with aloe vera and vinegar and used as a rinse with cool water, it helps cut through oil on scalp and leaves hair shiny.

GINSENG
Hair stimulant and toner.

GLUCOSE GLUTAMATE
Binds water-loving glucose molecules to the hair shaft, increasing suppleness.

GOLDENSEAL
Antiseptic; helps prevent dandruff and itchy scalp.

HENNA
Gives hair shine; smooths the hair shaft; untangles hair.

HOPS
Softens the hair and is a natural preservative. Promotes healthy cell growth.

HORSETAIL
Stimulates growth and combats dandruff.

JUNIPER
Helps control dandruff with an oily scalp.

MINT
Antiseptic. Nourishes and lubricates hair.

NETTLE
Calms scalp irritation and stimulates circulation to the scalp.

OLIVE OIL
Astringent and antiseptic for dry, dull hair.

PANTHENOL
Protects the hair; makes hair flexible and less brittle.

TEA TREE OIL
Helps control dandruff.

ROSEMARY
Conditions; stimulates circulation of blood to the scalp.

SAGE
Antimicrobial; hair toner.

WHEAT GERM OIL
Aids dry scalp by replacing natural oils lost during shampooing.

YARROW
Antiseptic; stimulates hair growth; fights dandruff.

ZINC
Helps control dandruff.

Chapter 4
ORGANICS

How To Buy Organic Foods

WHAT ARE ORGANIC FOODS?

Few sights are more beautiful than a colorful display of fresh fruits and vegetables. All those reds, greens, yellows and purples are a visual feast. Sustainably and organically produced foods are the centerpiece of most natural foods stores, and besides being visually appealing, they're good for the planet.

Sustainable agricultural methods encourage farmers to employ a variety of environmentally friendly practices. They include reducing the use of synthetic fertilizers, herbicides and pesticides; saving energy; conserving soil; maximizing irrigation; and controlling pests through as natural means as possible.

Organic farming is all that and more. Under organic methods, farmers combine old-world agricultural practices with the latest science to reduce or eliminate the use of synthetic chemicals. A common misconception is that organic farmers don't use pesticides. They do. Some of the pesticides, such as rotenone and pyrethrum, are botanical extracts that have been safely used by farmers since the 1800s. Others are natural minerals, such as sulphur, which is used to control fungus and mildew. A few, such as soap, are synthetic. The difference between pesticides used by organic farmers and those used by most other farmers is safety. The pesticides preferred by organic farmers break down into harmless ingredients more quickly and typically are applied before fruits and vegetables start growing or are used only in emergencies. It would be accurate to think of organic agriculture not as pesticide-free farming but as an all-encompassing production system that promotes environmentalism. Organic farmers use compost, manure and fish emulsions to build up the soil. They plant cover crops to help fix nutrients in the ground and prevent the dirt from washing or blowing away. They grow a wide variety of crops on their land to keep the soil from being depleted, discourage pests and encourage biodiversity.

Similar practices have enabled family farms in China to thrive for thousands of years, and while less than 5 percent of American farmers use organic methods, the number is growing quickly. One reason is that consumers are demanding it. Nearly half of all shoppers already buy organic foods at least occasionally, according to one survey. A 1988 report that Alar, a growth regulator once used on apples, can be harmful to children helped spark a 68 percent jump in the sales of organic produce the following year. The Organic Farming Research Foundation estimates that in the past few years exports of California organic produce have risen from $200,000 a year to $10 million. Another reason organic agriculture is receiving more attention is that growers see its advantages. Most major wineries, for example, have discovered that organic practices improve the flavor of grapes and boost harvests.

More and more organic foods also are processed by progressive factories that have extended the organic philosophy to their operations. They don't include chemicals in the food. Many retailers also contribute to the organic process by controlling pests with nonoffensive predators and pheromone traps. The traps use insects' own smells rather than toxic chemicals as a lure.

Take care in choosing organic wines

Not all wines labeled "organic" are organically grown *and* processed.

Although a wine might be made from organic grapes, it can contain added stabilizers and preservatives such as sulfites, bentonite and egg whites. Steven Frenkel, owner of Organic Vintages, a national distributor of organic wines, advises consumers to read labels carefully to determine whether an organic wine is organically processed as well as made from organically grown grapes. Look for "made without the use of added sulfites," or "naturally processed wine" on the label.

How to Choose Organic Foods
How do I know what to buy?

Organic foods were once confined mainly to fresh produce. Yet, a full range of processed organic foods is now available, from cheese and canned vegetables to beef and microwaveable dinners.

However, while natural foods stores try to sell only the highest quality products, not everything on the shelves will be sustainably or organically grown — everything we eat just isn't available everywhere throughout the year. As a result, many stores sell a mix of produce that comes from conventional, sustainable and organic farms. Signs explaining how the food was grown may be posted in the produce department. If it isn't, ask the department manager for help. Occasionally, retailers will stock "transitional" produce grown on farms that are switching to organic methods.

Because organic production standards vary widely throughout the United States, however, it's also important to know what growers, manufacturers and retailers mean when they claim something is organic. There's no nationwide law guaranteeing consumers that foods meet minimum standards before they're labeled organic (such laws are being written by the U.S. Department of Agriculture, but they probably won't be ready until 1995). Until these laws take effect, organic farming will continue to be regulated state by state — or not at all. Only 28 states have organic laws in place, and most aren't strict. California law, for instance, merely requires organic farmers to register with the state's agriculture department, which means consumers have to take the grower's word for it. To ensure the product is organic, check to see that it's certified by independent, third-party inspection organizations such as California Certified Organic Farmers (CCOF), Farm Verified Organic (FVO), the Organic Growers and Buyers Association (OGBA) and the Organic Crop Improvement Association (OCIA). These organizations enforce strict standards, including a requirement that growers stop using conventional methods for at least three years before their products can be certified organic.

> **Questions to consider before you shop**
>
> Consumer advocates say there are at least four questions you should ask yourself about the foods you buy:
>
> 1. Do they contain harmful amounts of pesticides or other synthetic chemicals?
> 2. Have any harmful ingredients — artificial colorings, flavorings or preservatives — been added to them?
> 3. Are they genetically altered, or do they contain any genetically altered ingredients?
> 4. Are they irradiated?
>
> If the answer to any of the questions is "yes," you should consider buying organic foods instead.

> ## *Organic foods are more nutritious*
> Organic fruits and vegetables are more nutritious than conventionally grown produce, research shows.
>
> Ounce for ounce, organic fruits and vegetables are twice as rich in some nutrients as comparable commercial products, according to a recent study reported in the *Journal of Applied Nutrition*.
>
> "This study has received a lot of attention because it's a possible answer to questions by nutritionists and other health care workers who ask what reason is behind the growing need for nutritional supplements," says Bob Smith, president of Doctor's Data Inc., who conducted the research. "Part of the answer may be commercial fruits and vegetables just aren't as good as they used to be."
>
> Researchers analyzed five fruits and vegetables over a two-year period for 22 nutrients and four toxic elements. The samples included pears, apples, sweet corn, wheat and potatoes. Organic sweet corn performed so much better than its conventional counterpart that it wasn't used in the calculations.
>
> Other studies have found that vine-ripened organic tomatoes contain more vitamin C than tomatoes that are picked green and artificially ripened with chemicals. Fruits and vegetables grown in rich soil also retain more trace minerals and other micronutrients than their conventional peers, research shows.

ENVIRONMENTAL REASONS TO BUY ORGANIC

More than 20,000 pesticides are registered for use in the United States. About 75 percent of the chemicals — some 2.2 billion pounds annually — are used on more than 900,000 U.S. farms at an annual cost of about $8.3 billion, according to the Pesticide Action Network. Pesticide sales have increased more than 2,700 percent since 1962, and U.S. users now account for one-third of the world pesticide market.

Touted as safe by the 120 leading producers of agricultural chemicals, pesticides have had a devastating effect on wildlife. DDT, for example, has killed millions of songbirds, eagles and hawks by weakening the shells of their eggs. Although DDT is now banned in many countries, other insecticides such as carbofuran and diazinon are thought to be responsible for the deaths of millions of birds in the United States alone each year. Groundwater contamination has spread the pollutants to the world's rivers, lakes and oceans, killing fish and aquatic plants.

Evidence is mounting that pesticides are harmful to humans, too. The environmental organization Greenpeace says "numerous studies show that many pesticides cause health problems ranging from such long-term chronic effects as cancer, genetic damage, birth defects, harm to the immune system, kidneys and liver, to short-term acute effects such as nerve damage, dizziness, nausea and fatigue." Some 27,000 to

300,000 U.S. farm workers are poisoned annually by pesticides, according to recent reports by the World Health Organization (WHO) and the U.S. government's General Accounting Office. Worldwide, about 25 million people are poisoned by farm chemicals every year — nearly 48 poisonings a minute — ending in more than 220,000 deaths, according to a 1989 report by the WHO/United Nations Environment Program. Inert ingredients in pesticides create additional health risks. Benzene and xylene, for example, have been linked to cancer. Some experts believe others, such as toluene, also can be toxic to fetuses. Sixty percent of all herbicides, 90 percent of all fungicides and 30 percent of all insecticides are considered carcinogenic by the Environmental Protection Agency (EPA). A 1987 National Academy of Sciences (NAS) report estimated that 20,000 cases of cancer a year can be linked to U.S. pesticide use.

"Pesticide residues pose a whole set of potential hazards," says consumer-interest attorney Jim Turner, author of *The Chemical Feast*. He cites EPA and NAS data to prove the point. The agency argues that cancer-causing pesticides pose only a "negligible risk" of no more than one death per 1 million people over a 70-year life span to food consumers. That translates into 260 deaths per pesticide use, he says. But since the EPA lists 86 pesticide uses, Turner says negligible means 34,480 deaths. "That's a number worth debating about," he says. The agency's risk analysis fails to account for multiple exposures or chemical interactions, he adds, noting that the risk may be much higher than the EPA believes.

Cancer-fighting vegetables

Carrots, sweet potatoes, yams, pumpkins, squash, kale, broccoli, cantaloupe.
CONTAINS: carotene.
ACTION: Neutralizes cancer-causing free radicals and singlet oxygen radicals; enhances immune system; reverses precancer conditions.

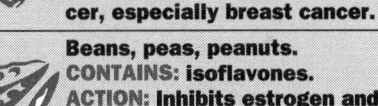

Cabbage, broccoli, cauliflower, mustard greens.
CONTAINS: indoles.
ACTION: Destroys estrogen, which has been linked to cancer, especially breast cancer.

Beans, peas, peanuts.
CONTAINS: isoflavones.
ACTION: Inhibits estrogen and estrogen receptors; destroys cancer gene enzymes.

Parsley.
CONTAINS: polyacetylene.
ACTION: Inhibits prostaglandins; destroys benzopyrene, a potent carcinogen.

Cucumbers.
CONTAINS: sterols.
ACTION: Decreases cholesterol.

Citrus fruits.
CONTAINS: terpenes.
ACTION: Increases enzymes known to break down carcinogens and decreases cholesterol.

Source: *Cancer & Nutrition* (Avery Publishing) by Charles B. Simone, M.D.

HEALTH REASONS TO EAT ORGANIC

Your mother knew what she was talking about when she told you to eat your vegetables.

The latest research shows that many fruits and vegetables are packed with nutrients that can help prevent cancer, heart disease and other illnesses. In addition to fiber, a known cancer fighter, fruits' and vegetables' beneficial nutrients include antioxidant vitamins such as C, A and E, the minerals selenium, zinc, copper and manganese, and other antioxidants such as beta-carotene. Studies show that people who eat lots of fruits and vegetables have about half the risk of developing most cancers compared to people who rarely include these foods in their diets.

Dark green leafy vegetables, broccoli, bok choy and figs are high in calcium, which is necessary for good bone formation. Dried fruits and potatoes are rich in iron. Citrus fruits contain vitamin C, as do strawberries, green peppers, melons, potatoes and broccoli. Apricots, cantaloupe, mango, papaya, carrots, kale, spinach, romaine lettuce, winter squash, sweet potatoes and tomatoes are high in vitamin A. For instance, a cup of cantaloupe provides 136 percent of the U.S. Recommended Daily Requirement for vitamin A and 100 percent of vitamin C.

Cruciferous vegetables, which get their name from the four-petaled crosslike flowers their plants produce, are rich in anticancer agents, according to the American Cancer Society (ACS) and the National Cancer Institute (NCI). Some common crucifers include broccoli, Brussels sprouts, kale, kohlrabi, mustard greens, turnips, radishes, cress, collards, cauliflower and cabbage. A cup of cooked collards, for instance, contains nearly 15,000 IUs of beta-carotene.

Unfortunately, a recent survey indicates that only one out of every five Americans eats at least the five servings a day of fruits and vegetables recommended by the NCI.

Taste the difference!

Many people believe organic produce looks and tastes better than conventionally grown produce. One reason may be that since it's grown in rich, nutritionally balanced soil, it "eats" a better diet and grows up healthier.

It's also usually picked and shipped when it's ripe, rather than while it's still green. The juicy, red, vine-ripened tomato is a symbol of farming methods that benefit the Earth and our palates.

Gourmet chefs such as Brother Ron Pickarski, an award-winning cook who specializes in vegetarian dishes, have celebrated the difference for decades by using organic produce in meals. "I... want to draw attention to food reforms that would alleviate world hunger and benefit the health of people and our planet," Pickarski says.

Eating Organic to Eliminate Additives From Your Diet

The average American consumes about five pounds of food additives a year, according to Michael Jacobson, Ph.D., executive director of the Center for Science in the Public Interest (CSPI), a consumer advocacy organization in Washington, D.C. "The good news is that the vast majority of the hundreds of chemicals that are added to our food are safe. The bad news is that some of them aren't but still haven't been banned from the food supply. And the other news is that some additives haven't been tested enough to determine whether they're safe or not," Jacobson says.

Children face the highest risk from additives, he adds. For instance, he says several studies show that artificial additives can trigger hyperactivity in young children. In a 1989 study, 24 hyperactive three- to six-year-old boys were fed specially prepared low-sugar, vitamin-rich diets that eliminated colorings, flavorings, monosodium glutamate (MSG), caffeine, preservatives and other substances. After four weeks, 10 of the boys showed a 45 percent behavioral improvement, four improved more modestly and 10 were unaffected. Some of the food additives considered questionable by CSPI include:

- **ARTIFICIAL COLORINGS**

Synthetic dyes have been suspected of being toxic or carcinogenic for decades, and many have been banned. For instance, Red No. 3 was banned for some — but not all — purposes by the Food and Drug Administration (FDA) because it caused thyroid tumors in mice. Yellow No. 5, America's second-most-popular food color, is associated with allergic reactions in some people including hives and severe breathing problems.

- **PRESERVATIVES**

BHA and BHT are two closely related chemicals that are added to oil-containing foods such as potato chips, cereals and bouillon cubes to prevent oxidation and retard rancidity. WHO's International Agency for Research on Cancer considers BHA to be a possible carcinogenic, and California officials have declared it carcinogenic. There are conflicting reports about BHT's effects, but it and BHA may be unnecessary additives since vitamins C and E are just as effective (but slightly more expensive) antioxidants.

- **MONOSODIUM GLUTAMATE**

MSG is a traditional Oriental additive that enhances the flavor of protein-containing foods. But too much of it reportedly causes headaches, tightness in the chest and burning sensations in the forearms and the back of the neck — the so-called "Chinese restaurant syndrome." Hydrolyzed vegetable protein (HVP) is a related additive that may contain MSG.

• NITRITES AND NITRATES

Sodium nitrite and sodium nitrate are two closely related chemicals used for centuries to preserve meat's color, enhance flavor and inhibit the growth of harmful bacteria. Nitrates and nitrites are considered harmless, but when combined with compounds called secondary amines, they form nitrosamines, extremely powerful cancer-causing chemicals. The chemical reaction occurs most readily at the high temperatures of frying (making nitrate-containing bacon a potential menace), but it may also occur in the warm environment of the stomach. The Japanese consume high levels of nitrites and suffer one of the highest rates of stomach cancer in the world.

• SULFITES

Sulfites are added to fruits and vegetables to stop them from turning brown, to freshly caught shrimp to control "black spot," and to wine to prevent discoloration and bacterial growth. However, sulfites can destroy vitamin B-1 (thiamine) and can provoke severe allergic reactions in some people.

Elude Irradiation

Approved by the FDA for use on fruits, vegetables and poultry, irradiation kills potentially hazardous bacteria and extends the shelf life of foods. (Irradiation involves exposing food to cobalt or cesium.) The nation's first irradiation facility opened in Florida in 1992 amidst controversy. Some researchers are concerned that irradiation may form cancer-causing compounds called unique radiolytic by-products and reduce the nutritional content of foods.

Escape Genetic Engineering

Genetic engineering is a revolutionary new food technology that splices genes from one species into another to improve certain qualities or uses chemicals to mutate genes to achieve new results. Tomatoes have been spliced with fish genes, for instance, to allow them to ripen on the vine yet resist crushing during shipment. Pork has been spliced with human genes to boost weight gain in pigs.

Genetic engineering has received blanket approval from the FDA even though its safety is virtually untested. Manufacturers won't even have to say the foods have been genetically altered on their labels. "We think this technology... is simply inappropriate in the food chain," says Ted Howard, executive director of the Pure Food Campaign. "This technology is breaking down the barriers between plants, animals and humans. Do we have the wisdom to govern a technology that allows us to direct and design life and ultimately the process of evolution on this planet? I think the jury is still very much out on that question."

ECONOMIC REASONS TO BUY ORGANIC
Organic foods are less costly in the long run

Organic foods sometimes cost more than conventionally grown foods, but the latter contain many hidden costs — from billions of dollars in federal farm subsidies that rarely benefit organic farmers to the cost of cleaning up environmental damage caused by farm chemicals.

According to a recent Cornell University study, some of the annual environmental costs include:

Damage to agricultural ecosystems	Pesticide poisonings and related illnesses	Pesticide regulation and monitoring	Testing drinking water for pesticide contamination
$525 million.	$250 million.	$150 million.	$1.3 billion.

None of these figures begins to calculate the cost of long-term environmental damage of farm chemicals to the air, water and soil. "Farmers make no allowance for wear and tear when it comes to their most valuable assets — natural resources such as soil and water," notes Mohammed El-Ashry, senior vice president of the World Resource Institute. "Ruining natural assets costs money just as surely as new barns or tractors do, so ignoring resources is irrational. Farmers will pay in terms of lost productivity, but the larger cost to the environment will eventually be borne by the nation as a whole."

"These costs are real," adds Paul Faeth, an institute researcher. "Just because we don't account for them doesn't mean they don't happen."

Author and radio talk-show host Gary Null says that if all the costs of producing a head of lettuce under conventional means were counted, it would add up to $3.

Richard Reed, spokesman for the Community Alliance for Family Farmers, urges shoppers to treat each dollar as a powerful vote for a sustainable food production system. "When I buy organic food," he says, "it has an immediate impact on the rural environment. It might cost me several hundred dollars more a year, but I feel I'm making a donation to my favorite charity — the land."

> **IN SEEKING TO EAT WELL AND BE A RESPONSIBLE CITIZEN, EDUCATE YOURSELF ABOUT HOW THE FOODS YOU EAT GET TO YOUR TABLE AND WHETHER OR NOT THEY WERE PRODUCED SUSTAINABLY. STOP THINKING ONLY ABOUT YOUR OWN HEALTH AND START THINKING ABOUT THE HEALTH OF THE PLANET.**
>
> —Joan Dye Gussow, nutrition professor at Columbia University and author of *Chicken Little, Tomato Sauce & Agriculture* (Japan Publications)

Three Great Reasons to Buy Organic Foods

1. Do It for Our Future — "We have not inherited the Earth from our fathers, we are borrowing it from our children," says Lester Brown, author of *Building a Sustainable Society*. It's estimated that the average child receives four times more exposure than an adult to at least eight widely used cancer-causing pesticides in food. The EPA considers 60 percent of all herbicides, 90 percent of all fungicides and 30 percent of all insecticides carcinogenic. The 1987 National Academy of Sciences report *Regulating Pesticides in Food* estimated that pesticides may cause an extra 1.4 million cancer cases among Americans over their lifetimes. That knowledge can sour even the most pleasurable nonorganic eating experience.

2. Protect Our Soil, Water and Air — Soil is the foundation of the food chain in organic farming, so organic farmers enrich it naturally rather than rely on chemical fertilizers. Chemical-dependent agricultural practices contribute to the annual erosion of 3 billion tons of topsoil from U.S. farmland — seven times faster than it's being built up. The practice of planting the same crops year after year makes them more susceptible to pests, continuing the vicious pesticide cycle. Some farm chemicals wash into our water. The EPA has found 98 different pesticides including DDT in groundwater in 48 states, contaminating the drinking water of more than 10 million people. Conventional farms also are heavily dependent on fossil fuels. Fertilizers, pesticides, tractors, transportation and processing all consume valuable resources and pollute the air; more energy is used to produce synthetic fertilizers than is used in tilling, cultivating and harvesting all the crops in the United States. However, organic farming is predominantly based on labor-intensive practices such as hand weeding and using green manures to build the soil.

3. Help Small Farmers — Although more and more corporate farms are converting to organic methods, most organic farms are family farms of less than 100 acres. In the past decade, the United States has lost more than 650,000 family farms, according to the Texas Department of Agriculture. Yet, because natural food stores tend to buy their produce locally, you can help save family farms. Organic farming also is safer for farm workers. It's estimated that 27,000 to 300,000 U.S. farm workers are poisoned annually by pesticides. Two studies by the NCI found that farmers exposed to herbicides have a three to six times greater risk than nonfarmers of contracting a specific type of cancer. Worldwide, some 25 million people a year are poisoned by pesticides, with 222,000 deaths.

Chapter 5
BULK FOODS
How To Buy Bulk & Packaged Foods

NATURAL FOODS: A WEALTH OF GOOD TASTES

So many natural foods are available today, it's impossible to name them all here let alone describe their benefits. They range from pure bottled waters and sugar-free desserts to simple bulk grains and elaborate frozen TV dinners. One thing they all have in common is their use of wholesome, nutritious, basic ingredients — beans, whole grains and pastas, fruits and vegetables.

Think of a conventional food, and you'll probably find a tastier, more nutritious and healthier counterpart at your local natural products store. In fact, many lasting food trends began in natural products stores. Yogurt and fruit-only jams, for instance, were health-oriented products that spread from natural products stores to conventional supermarkets as consumer demand for them grew.

Often, natural foods convey the same health benefits as their conventional peers while avoiding harmful effects. Fat-free foods, for instance, may be quite different in a natural products store versus a supermarket. While some fat substitutes are combinations of naturally occurring ingredients such as plant gums or starches, others are the products of high-tech processes and chemicals with questionable health effects.

Use this chapter as your guide to staple foods as well as to ingredients of the legions of pre-prepared, pre-packaged natural foods now available.

> ❝❝ GRAINS CONTAIN ALL THE MAJOR NUTRIENT GROUPS NEEDED BY THE BODY—CARBOHYDRATES, PROTEIN, FATS, VITAMINS AND MINERALS. ❞❞
> —Rebecca Wood, author of *Quinoa— The Supergrain* (The Bootstrap Press)

ENVIRONMENTAL REASONS TO EAT NATURAL FOODS

Eating low on the food chain with foods that use a wide variety of natural beans, grains and pastas is not only good for the body, but also for the planet. Among other things, such foods:
- Reduce our reliance on livestock, which can deplete enormous land and water resources.
- Promote biological diversity by encouraging farmers to grow a wide variety of foods, many of which have been sorely neglected by agriculture's focus on wheat, corn and other major crops.
- Discourage monocropping, the repeated planting and harvesting of single crops that increases farmers' reliance on chemical pesticides, fertilizers and herbicides.

Many natural foods help the planet in other ways, too. Fruits, nuts and oils harvested from South American rain forests, for example, provide an ongoing source of income to workers there and give companies and governments economic incentives to prevent deforestation.

ECONOMIC REASONS TO BUY BEANS, GRAINS & PASTA

It's hard to beat the economic value of beans, grains and pasta. Even a ready-to-eat food such as tofu or tempeh made from soybeans usually costs less than $1.50 a pound, much less than most meats or fish. Bulk foods are an even better bargain because they save money on packaging.

Given that beans, grains and pasta can be used in a wide variety of delicious and highly nutritious recipes — from soups and sauces to stir-fries and stews — they're the undisputed foods of choice for thrifty chefs.

HEALTH REASONS TO EAT WHOLE FOODS

One out of every three children born in 1994 is likely to have a serious heart attack or stroke before the age of 60. The major culprit? High blood cholesterol from meat and dairy foods.

Too much cholesterol in the blood leads to a gradual buildup of fatty deposits on the walls of the arteries. Over the years, this buildup can block arteries completely (a condition known as atherosclerosis), resulting in heart attack, stroke or a related disease.

High blood cholesterol isn't usually a condition a child outgrows. It stays high and increases with age unless something is done about it. One major step you can take to protect yourself and your children is to eat more complex carbohydrates including fruits, vegetables, beans, whole grains and pastas found in the bulk and packaged sections of natural foods stores. Because such foods are rich in vitamins, minerals and other nutrients but contain little or no fat (and no cholesterol), many nutrition experts believe they should make up at least 55 percent of your diet.

"It's hard to get fat — or stay fat — on this type of diet," notes Nava Atlas, author of *Vegetarian Celebrations: Menus for the Holidays and Other Festive Occasions.*

As an added plus, beans and whole grains and pasta are high in fiber, which not only enhances their ability to prevent heart disease, but also may help prevent other illnesses such as colon cancer, diverticulosis and diabetes. The typical American eats 10 to 15 grams of fiber a day, but the National Cancer Institute recommends a daily consumption of 25 to 35 grams — equivalent to approximately six servings of whole grains, bread, cereal or legumes and four servings of fresh fruit and vegetables.

Gourmet Grain Guide

AMARANTH

Characteristics: Technically not a grain but a cereal-like herb, this tiny seed was an important food source in the ancient Aztec culture and is so nutritionally rich that it once was named one of the world's most promising foods by the National Academy of Sciences. Creamy beige color and wild, woodsy flavor. Texture of cooked grain is similar to cornmeal mush. Amaranth is gluten free. It's also high in protein, calcium, phosphorus, iron and fiber, as well as the essential amino acids lysine and methionine, which often are lacking in grains.

Uses & Cooking Instructions: Found in cereal, pasta, bread, cookies and other baked goods. Amaranth flour can be substituted for up to one-fourth the wheat flour in baked goods. Cooked amaranth may be eaten as a hot cereal, combined with other grains or added to bread, muffin and pancake batters. Becomes translucent as it cooks. To prepare, add 1 cup amaranth to 1-1/2 to 2-1/2 cups boiling water. Cook 20 minutes. Add salt to taste after cooking. Yields 2 cups.

BUCKWHEAT

Characteristics: Not a true grain, but the seeds of a plant related to rhubarb. Hulled, toasted buckwheat, or "kasha," is available whole and cracked. Reddish-brown color and robust, earthy flavor. Consistency of cooked kasha is soft and fluffy. Contains high-quality protein, vitamin E, B vitamins, iron and calcium. Gluten free.

Uses & Cooking Instructions: Found in pasta and pancake mixes. Cooked kasha is excellent in pilafs, stuffings, croquettes, burgers and knishes or combined with potatoes, vegetables or pasta. To prepare, add 1 cup buckwheat to 2 cups boiling salted water. Cover and cook 10 to 12 minutes. Yields 3-1/2 cups.

KAMUT

Characteristics: A distant relative of wheat, this ancient Egyptian grain contains 40 percent more protein than modern hybridized wheat and may be less allergenic than modern strains. Whole kernels resemble large, golden grains of rice. Rich, buttery flavor; chewy texture. Also available in oatmeal-like rolled flakes.

Uses & Cooking Instructions: Found in ready-to-eat cereal and pasta. Kamut flour may be substituted for wheat flour in most recipes. Use cooked whole grain in salads and pilafs and instead of brown rice in most dishes. To prepare, soak 1 cup kamut overnight in cold water. Drain and add to 3 cups boiling, salted water. Cook 30 to 40 minutes. Yields 2 cups.

MILLET

Characteristics: Small, yellow, beadlike grain containing high-quality protein. In the United States, millet is commonly associated with bird food; however, in Africa, China and India, it's a dietary staple. A good source of potassium, magnesium, phosphorus and B vitamins, millet is less allergenic than wheat and corn and naturally alkaline, which means it's easy to digest. Cooked whole millet has a mild, nutty flavor and fluffy texture.

Uses & Cooking Instructions: Found in ready-to-eat cereal and bread. Cooked whole millet is delicious in salads, pilafs and croquettes or tossed with pasta. Combine with vegetables in a spicy curry or red pepper sauce. Add cooked millet to muffin and pancake batters. To prepare, add 1 cup millet to 2 cups boiling salted water. Cook 30 minutes. Yields 4 cups.

QUINOA (PRONOUNCED "KEEN-WA")

Characteristics: Actually an herb, this small, disk-shaped seed was once a staple of the Inca culture. Those who are allergic to wheat or corn will likely find this grain easy to digest; quinoa contains 50 percent more protein than other grains, as well as higher levels of calcium, phosphorus, iron and B vitamins. Color of whole quinoa ranges from creamy beige to black. Light taste and delicate, fluffy texture.

Uses & Cooking Instructions: Found in ready-to-eat cereal and pasta. Quinoa flour may be substituted for one-fourth the wheat flour in most baked goods. Try cooked, whole quinoa in salads, soups, stews, pilafs, croquettes, burgers and as a substitute for rice. Especially tasty in Mexican and Indian dishes. Quinoa must be rinsed thoroughly before cooking to remove its bitter, soaplike coating. Becomes translucent when cooked. To prepare, add 1 cup quinoa to 2 cups boiling salted water. Cover and simmer 15 minutes. Yields 3-1/2 cups.

SPECIALTY RICES (BASMATI, JASMINE, JAPONICA, WEHANI)

Characteristics: These aromatic and colorful varieties of rice are delicious alternatives to ordinary brown rice.

Uses & Cooking Instructions: Use instead of brown rice in any recipe. Brown basmati and jasmine are especially good with Thai and India curries as well as Oriental stir-fries. Wehani and japonica blends make excellent stuffings and pilafs. Prepare all varieties as you would brown rice. Add 1 cup rice to 2 cups boiling, salted water. Cover and cook 45 minutes. Yields 3 cups.

Shopping at the Bean Boutique
Beans are a remarkable food.

Nutrients that are plentiful in beans include vitamins A and C, B vitamins, calcium, phosphorus, potassium and iron. One cup of cooked beans contains 5 to 7 grams of usable protein and less than 1 gram of fat (one exception is soybeans, which have 15 grams of fat per 1 cup serving). Beans and grains combined provide complete protein, which makes them an excellent alternative to meat.

Remember when buying beans that 1 pound measures about 2 cups and yields 6 cups of cooked beans. Dried beans will keep up to a year if stored in an airtight container at room temperature. Dried beans must be soaked first to decrease cooking time and reduce gas-causing substances. Here's how:

1 Place beans in a large saucepan with three to four times as much water.

2 Bring to a boil and cook 2 to 3 minutes. Remove from heat, cover and set aside 1 to 4 hours. The longer beans soak, the more gases dissolve.

3 Discard soaking water. Drain and rinse beans. Return soaked, rinsed beans to saucepan with fresh water. Water level should be one inch above beans.

4 You can add a tablespoon of cooking oil to reduce foaming and boil-overs.

5 Boil beans for 10 minutes, then simmer until tender (about 1 to 2 hours).

6 Add seasonings during cooking, if desired. Add acidic ingredients such as tomatoes or vinegar, which retard cooking, after the beans are tender.

7 A pressure cooker with a clog-proof vent cuts cooking time in half and allows you to skip presoaking.

ADSUKI (AZUKI, ADUKI)
Small, oval, burgundy-colored bean with a white stripe. Native to the Orient. Easy to digest. Delicate, sweet flavor and soft texture. Use in soups, salads, Oriental stir-fries, bean cakes and pasta dishes. Combines well with winter squash, sweet red pepper and brown rice. Season with tamari, ginger or Chinese five spice.

ANASAZI
Red-and-white speckled bean originally cultivated by Native Americans. Loses mottled appearance during cooking. Size and shape similar to pinto bean. Sweet, full flavor and mealy texture. Excellent in Mexican dishes. Use for refried beans, burritos and bean dips. Season with garlic, chilies, cumin or coriander.

BLACK (TURTLE)
Small, round, purple-black bean. A staple of Latin America and the Orient. Distinct earthy taste and mealy texture. Excellent in Mexican, Caribbean and

Southwestern dishes. Use in sauces, soups, bean cakes, refried beans, salads and bean dips. Combines well with tomatoes, corn, avocado, rice and other grains. Season with garlic, lime juice, chilies, cumin or fresh cilantro.

CHICKPEA (GARBANZO)
Medium-sized, round, tan bean with a nutlike flavor and firm texture. Popular in Middle Eastern and Mediterranean cooking. Often used in dips (such as hummus), soups, salads, croquettes (falafel), curries and pasta dishes. Season with olive oil, garlic, lemon juice, parsley or rosemary.

FAVA (BROAD)
Large, flat, kidney-shaped bean. Light brown color. Strong, almost bitter flavor and granular texture. Popular in the Middle East and Italy. Use in soups, stews and casseroles. Combines well with tomatoes, sweet bell pepper and Parmesan cheese. Season with garlic, chilies and cumin.

LENTIL
Small, disk-shaped seed. May be yellow, red, green or brown. Delicate, earthy flavor and creamy texture. Use in soups, salads, purees, dips, pâtés, burgers and curries. Season with garlic, onion, thyme or curry.

MUNG
Small, oblong, dark olive bean native to India. Delicate, sweet flavor and soft texture. Easy to digest. Use in Indian dals and curries. Sprouted mung beans are popular in Oriental and Asian cooking. Season with curry, tamari or ginger.

PINTO
Oval, pink-and-brown speckled bean native to Mexico. Color fades to brown during cooking. Full-bodied, earthy flavor and mealy texture. Great for Tex-Mex dishes. Often used in refried beans and chili. Season with garlic, onions, chilies and cumin.

SMALL RED (MEXICAN RED)
Dark red bean similar to the kidney bean only smaller. Rich sweet flavor and mealy texture. Holds shape during cooking. Most often used in soups, salads, chili, refried beans and Creole dishes. Substitute for kidney or pinto beans in any recipe. Season with garlic, onion, chilies and cumin.

SOY
Pea-shaped bean native to Central China. May be yellow, green, brown or black. Mild nutty flavor and firm texture. Commonly used to make tofu, tempeh, tamari, soybeans also are great in soups, stews, salads, burgers and Boston baked beans. Season with garlic, ginger and tamari.

WHITE (CANNELLINI, GREAT NORTHERN, NAVY)
Oblong, cream-colored beans of varying sizes. Mild flavor, slightly granular texture. Interchangeable in most recipes. Use in soups, stews, casseroles and Boston baked. Cannellini are delectable in Italian-style salads and pasta dishes. Season with garlic, rosemary and oregano.

An International Guide to Pasta & Noodles

ARTICHOKE

Characteristics: A blend of semolina or whole wheat flour and Jerusalem artichoke flour; or just Jerusalem artichoke flour in a wheat-free version. The flour made from Jerusalem artichokes (the roots of a plant related to the sunflower) is a low-calorie bulking agent that promotes healthy digestion. Jerusalem artichoke pasta is mild and flavorful, with a pleasant texture. Available in standard shapes such as angel hair, shells, elbows and fettucine, and gourmet flavors such as garlic-parsley and tomato basil.

Suggested Uses: In Italian-style recipes, especially with light, fresh tomato sauces and pestos; use small shapes in pasta salads, macaroni and cheese casserole; combine with beans in hot or cold dishes.

BROWN RICE

Characteristics: Made from brown rice flour, which has excellent digestibility, nearly complete range of B-complex vitamins and a significant amount of vitamin E. While certainly a boon to the wheat intolerant, this cooks to a consistency and flavor more akin to mashed rice than to pasta and is rather sticky. Elbow shapes are most common.

Suggested Uses: Because of sticky texture, best used in casseroles combined with beans, vegetable and/or cheeses or as a side dish similar to rice pudding with sweetener, raisins and cinnamon.

SOY

Characteristics: Soy pasta combines whole wheat flour with 10 to 20 percent soy flour and comes in a variety of shapes. Soy flour is rich in complete, high-quality protein and high in the B-complex vitamins and vitamin E. The flavor and texture of soy pasta are smoother than 100 percent whole wheat pasta.

Suggested Uses: Use shaped pastas as substitutes for similarly shaped ordinary pastas in salads, casseroles, soups and stew.

SESAME-RICE

Characteristics: Made from 80 percent whole durum wheat (semolina) and 10 percent each rice flour and sesame flour. This pasta, available most commonly in spiral shapes, has a nice, nutty flavor.

Suggested Uses: In pasta salads, hot or cold with tender-crisp vegetables and soy-flavored vinaigrette; with pesto sauce; in casseroles; with fresh tomato sauce; as a substitute for spirals in Italian-style dishes; toss with steamed vegetables and beans or tofu; in stews.

QUINOA

Characteristics: These noodles, combining a great percentage of whole wheat flour with the flour of quinoa, the super-nutritious, high-protein ancient grain, come primarily in the form of flat fettucine noodles. The nutty flavor of quinoa comes through lightly in the pasta.

Suggested Uses: Substitute fettucine-shaped noodles for ordinary fettucine in Italian-style dishes; with creamy milk or soy milk-based sauce; with steamed fresh greens such as kale or spinach. Serve quinoa-corn elbows as a simple side dish with soy margarine; use in macaroni salad, macaroni and cheese casserole.

UDON
Characteristics: Long, somewhat thick noodles akin to linguine. The whole wheat variety of this Japanese import that's available in natural products stores has a smooth texture and mild flavor.

Suggested Uses: Substitute for ordinary spaghetti with pesto or miso-based sauces; serve with diced tofu or tempeh, scallions, and soy sauce; with ginger-flavored dressing and crisp vegetables.

VEGETABLE
Characteristics: Natural products stores play host to a variety of pastas that combine whole or refined durum wheat flour with vegetable flours. Spinach pasta is perhaps the most widely used and imparts the most pronounced flavor. One cup of cooked spinach pasta supplies 25 percent of the RDA for vitamin A. Beet, carrot and tomato pastas are also common. Available in spirals, shells, and elbows, often in packages of mixed colors.

Suggested Uses: With light sauces such as garlic and olive oil or pureed fresh tomato sauce; particularly good in cold marinated salads with a light vinaigrette.

LUPINI
Characteristics: This specialty pasta is made from whole wheat flour and sweet lupin, a legume that's high in protein and fiber. Unlike other pastas, lupini contains a significant amount of beta-carotene and is rich in amino acids and a wide range of minerals. This pasta, available in spaghetti or small shapes, has a grainy texture, deep brown color and assertive flavor.

Suggested Uses: Combine with small shapes with crunchy vegetables such as carrots, cauliflower and broccoli in hearty salad; in casseroles, winter soups and stews. Serve simply with olive oil, garlic and Parmesan cheese or soy Parmesan.

BUCKWHEAT (SOBA)
Characteristics: A spaghetti-shaped noodle combining hearty-tasting buckwheat flour with wheat or whole wheat flour. Buckwheat is high in protein, iron, phosphorus,

potassium and B vitamins, and it's one of the best grain sources of calcium. Pasta comes in varying percentages of buckwheat, from 20 percent buckwheat/80 percent whole wheat to 100 percent buckwheat, which is wheat free.

Suggested Uses: With sweet-sour sauces and stir-fried Oriental vegetables; substitute for ordinary spaghetti; break into shorter lengths for soups and broths; serve simply with soy sauce and sesame oil.

BUCKWHEAT VARIATIONS (JINENJO, LOTUS ROOT, MUGWORT)

Characteristics: These soba noodles contain a mixture of wheat and buckwheat flour plus the ingredient for which they are named: Jinenjo is a wild mountain yam; lotus root is the root of the pond lotus; and mugwort is an herb. These ingredients are prized in the Orient for their medicinal and nutritional values. All of these noodles are spaghetti shaped and delicately flavored.

Suggested Uses: With spicy peanut sauce; in salads combined with Oriental vegetables such as snow peas, daikon radish, mung bean sprouts and soy-flavored vinaigrette; plus all other uses for buckwheat noodles.

SOMEN

Characteristics: These spaghetti-shaped noodles are imported from Japan, where they're traditionally eaten cold during the summer months. A smooth-textured whole wheat version is available in natural foods stores.

Suggested Uses: Following Japanese tradition, serve cold with crisp matchstick vegetables such as daikon radish, carrot and turnip in light soy vinaigrette; substitute for ordinary spaghetti with spicy peanut or sesame sauce.

Oil Know-How

Most conventional grocery stores focus on one type of oil—cooking oil from corn or a blend of vegetable sources. However, natural products stores feature many different types of natural oils that play a crucial role in a well-balanced diet, says Ann Louise Gittleman, M.S., author of *Supernutrition for Women*.

Oils usually are chosen according to cooking needs, but because they perform a wide variety of nutritional tasks, Gittleman says you might consider selecting your oil based upon particular health needs. If weight loss is your goal, for instance, then safflower oil, the oil highest in fat-burning linoleic acid, may be the oil for you. Worried about cholesterol? Then you might try rice bran oil, which, according to the latest research, is beneficial for controlling cholesterol levels.

Natural oils also are made differently than their conventional peers, which may be extracted with damaging high heat and/or chemical solvents before they're bleached, deodorized and laced with preservatives for uniformity. True cold-pressed oils are pressed with little or no heat to preserve their nutritional value. To make expeller-pressed oils, cooked raw material such as soybeans or corn is pressed through an expeller or screw press at the lowest possible temperature. Unrefined oils, which have a stronger odor and flavor than other oils, undergo only the initial pressing steps. Hydrogenation is a chemical process that makes liquid vegetable oils more saturated, or solid, to make them last longer or give them a buttery (and therefore potentially artery-clogging) texture.

Here's a brief guide to some popular natural oils:

FLAX OIL
High source of Omega-3 fatty acids for improving cardiovascular, immune, nerve and reproductive function. Use in no-heat dishes; drizzle onto popcorn, cereals and veggies. Refrigerate up to three weeks.

SAFFLOWER OIL
Aids in weight loss and alleviates hunger. Use in no-heat dishes and salad dressings. Refrigerate.

SESAME OIL
Contains antirancidity factors. Use in dressings, stir-fries and soups. Store in a cool, dry place.

OLIVE OIL
May lower cholesterol levels because it's rich in heart-healthy monounsaturates. Use in dressings, sauces, sautés. Store in a cool, dry place.

CANOLA OIL
Rich in monounsaturates. Use in baking, sautéing and sauces. Store in a cool, dry place.

SOY OIL
Good for nerves and memory. Use for light sautéing, pressure cooking. Refrigerate.

How Sweet It Is: Sweet-tooth Alternatives

Desserts are some of the most sought-after foods in natural products stores — not just because they taste great, but because they tend to shun artificial flavorings, colorings and preservatives and embrace wholesome ingredients such as alternative sweeteners to refined white sugar.

The average American consumes 125 pounds of highly refined white sugar each year. White sugar is extracted from sugar cane or sugar beets with chemicals and is 99.8 percent sucrose. Because it lacks fiber and is a simple carbohydrate, refined white sugar is quickly absorbed by the body. The pancreas and adrenal glands may overreact as a result, lowering blood sugar levels and causing fatigue and irritability. Refined white sugar contains no nutrients other than simple carbohydrates and actually robs the body of vitamins and minerals as it's metabolized. It's also been linked to obesity, diabetes, hypoglycemia, tooth decay and other health problems.

Conventional sugar replacements include saccharin, which has been linked to cancer, and aspartame, a combination of the amino acids aspartic acid and phenylalanine. Although aspartame is low in calories and the FDA believes it's safe, some scientists suspect aspartame adversely affects the neurotransmitters in the brain that control moods, thinking and behavior. There is concern that it also may contribute to mental retardation in babies, as well as other serious problems in adults such as headaches and seizures. The FDA has received more complaints about adverse health effects of aspartame than for any food ingredient in the agency's history.

Although no sweetener is perfect, some are better for your health than others. Here's a brief guide to some popular alternative sweeteners that may be used in natural products:

❑ **Amazake** — A thick, puddinglike, whole-grain sweet beverage made from organic brown rice. The rice is cooked into a porridge and then injected with koji, the *Aspergillus oryzae* culture that is also used to make miso, shoyu and rice vinegar. It's about 21 percent sugar, mainly glucose and maltose (malt sugar) and is high in carbohydrates and other nutrients, including vitamin B and iron.

❑ **Barley Malt Syrup or Powder** — A natural high-carbohydrate grain sweetener with a rich, malty flavor. Made from soaked, sprouted or hot-air-dried barley combined with water and cooked into a thick, sweet syrup. Because it's absorbed slowly, it has a less extreme effect on blood sugar levels than refined sweeteners.

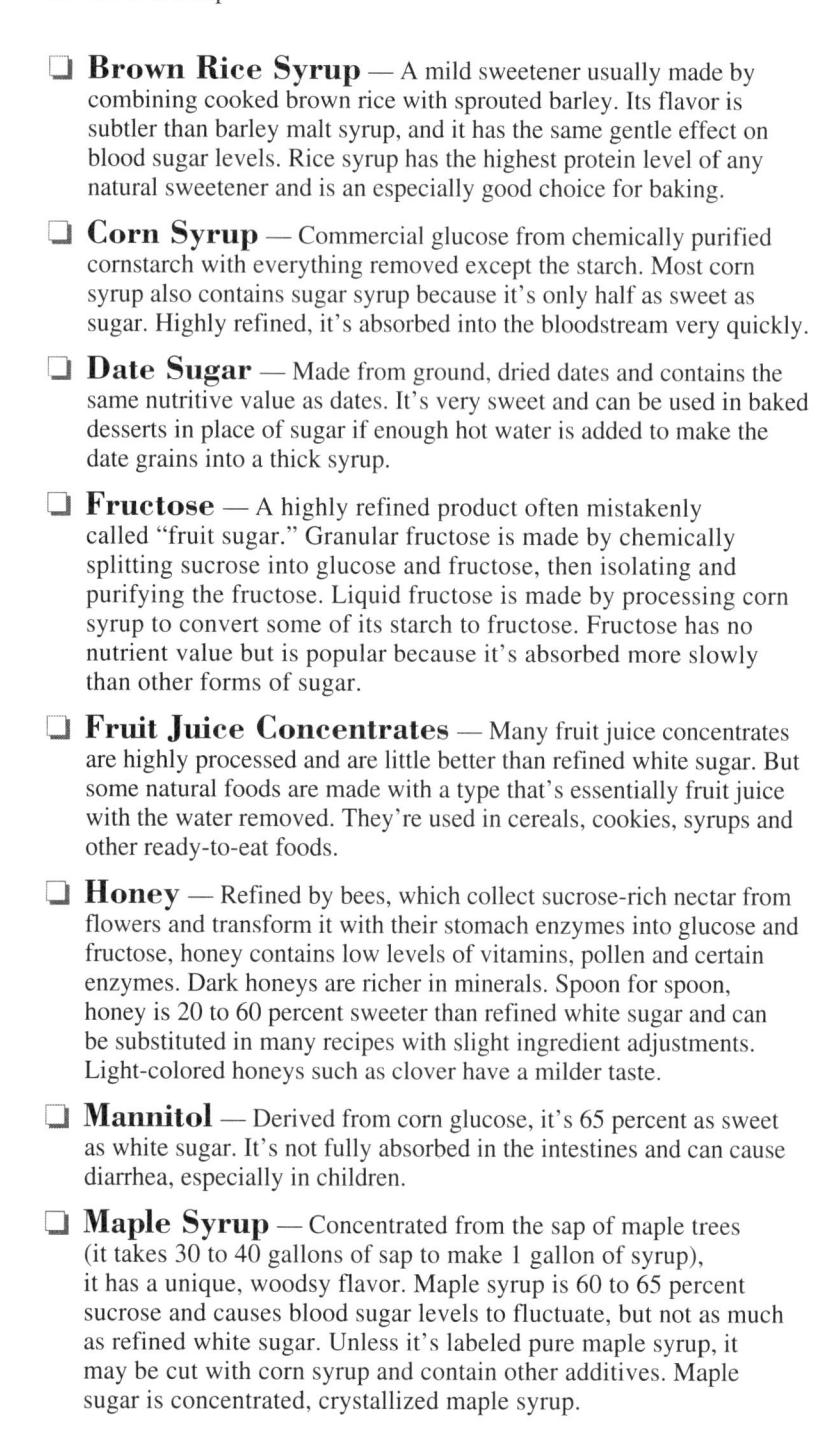

- **Brown Rice Syrup** — A mild sweetener usually made by combining cooked brown rice with sprouted barley. Its flavor is subtler than barley malt syrup, and it has the same gentle effect on blood sugar levels. Rice syrup has the highest protein level of any natural sweetener and is an especially good choice for baking.

- **Corn Syrup** — Commercial glucose from chemically purified cornstarch with everything removed except the starch. Most corn syrup also contains sugar syrup because it's only half as sweet as sugar. Highly refined, it's absorbed into the bloodstream very quickly.

- **Date Sugar** — Made from ground, dried dates and contains the same nutritive value as dates. It's very sweet and can be used in baked desserts in place of sugar if enough hot water is added to make the date grains into a thick syrup.

- **Fructose** — A highly refined product often mistakenly called "fruit sugar." Granular fructose is made by chemically splitting sucrose into glucose and fructose, then isolating and purifying the fructose. Liquid fructose is made by processing corn syrup to convert some of its starch to fructose. Fructose has no nutrient value but is popular because it's absorbed more slowly than other forms of sugar.

- **Fruit Juice Concentrates** — Many fruit juice concentrates are highly processed and are little better than refined white sugar. But some natural foods are made with a type that's essentially fruit juice with the water removed. They're used in cereals, cookies, syrups and other ready-to-eat foods.

- **Honey** — Refined by bees, which collect sucrose-rich nectar from flowers and transform it with their stomach enzymes into glucose and fructose, honey contains low levels of vitamins, pollen and certain enzymes. Dark honeys are richer in minerals. Spoon for spoon, honey is 20 to 60 percent sweeter than refined white sugar and can be substituted in many recipes with slight ingredient adjustments. Light-colored honeys such as clover have a milder taste.

- **Mannitol** — Derived from corn glucose, it's 65 percent as sweet as white sugar. It's not fully absorbed in the intestines and can cause diarrhea, especially in children.

- **Maple Syrup** — Concentrated from the sap of maple trees (it takes 30 to 40 gallons of sap to make 1 gallon of syrup), it has a unique, woodsy flavor. Maple syrup is 60 to 65 percent sucrose and causes blood sugar levels to fluctuate, but not as much as refined white sugar. Unless it's labeled pure maple syrup, it may be cut with corn syrup and contain other additives. Maple sugar is concentrated, crystallized maple syrup.

- **Molasses** — About 35 to 70 percent sucrose, it's made either as an end product or as a by-product of making white sugar. It's very high in minerals but has only half the sweetening power of white table sugar. The by-product is called blackstrap molasses and can contain sulphur dioxide, which causes allergic reactions in some people.
- **Sorbitol** — Derived from corn glucose as is mannitol, it's 60 percent as sweet as white sugar. It's absorbed slowly and is used in foods for diabetics because it needs little, if any, insulin to digest. It doesn't promote tooth decay but can cause diarrhea.
- **Sorghum Molasses** — The concentrated juice of the sweet sorghum plant, a cereal grain. It tastes similar to molasses but has a lighter, fruitier flavor. It's about 65 percent sucrose and retains some minerals and vitamins.
- **Stevia Leaf** — A noncaloric herbal sweetener that has been grown and used in South America since antiquity. It's 100 to 200 times sweeter than white sugar and was safely used for more than a decade in the United States and since the 1970s in Japan, where an extract of the leaf is widely used in a variety of products including, at one time, diet sodas. The FDA banned stevia imports in the late 1980s claiming that it's an "unsafe food additive" — a point that's hotly disputed by herbalists, who note that stevia, like many culinary herbs, has a long history of safe use as a food and is exempt from food additive regulations.
- **Sucanat** — A brand name for organically grown dehydrated cane juice, which is extracted mechanically rather than chemically, then dried. The average sugar content is 85 percent, and all of the complex sugars, vitamins, minerals, amino acids and molasses are retained. Sucanat was created by a Swiss pediatrician who noted in the 1950s that cavities were becoming much more common among children whose diets included white sugar and refined foods such as white bread. Yet sugar cane harvesters, who swallow an average of 1 liter of cane juice a day as they chew cane stalks to quench their thirst, have very healthy teeth, according to several studies. Researchers believe one factor may be trace elements in unrefined cane juice that help neutralize cavity-causing mouth acids.
- **Turbinado Sugar** — Refined white sugar before the final refining to extract molasses.
- **Xylitol** — Derived from birchwood chips, it has been shown to reduce cavities by neutralizing mouth acids. It's as sweet as fructose, but a 1977 English study raised questions as to whether it could cause bladder cancers, and the FDA has considered banning it.

Chapter 6
MEATS & DAIRY

How To Shop For Natural Meats & Dairy Products

HEALTH REASONS TO EAT NATURAL MEATS & DAIRY PRODUCTS

If you're going to include protein-rich meat and dairy products in your diet, then the natural alternatives available in health food stores offer some definite advantages over conventional products.

Organically produced dairy products, for instance, almost certainly are purer than their conventional counterparts. According to a recent report by the U.S. government's General Accounting Office (GAO), federal and state agencies can't prove the safety of the nation's milk supply through existing drug residue testing programs. More than 170 million gallons of milk — about 1 percent of the supply — had to be discarded in 1991 due to drug residue contamination. However, the GAO says "the actual extent of contamination is probably greater" because tests are conducted for only four of the 82 potentially dangerous drugs used on dairy cows.

To make matters worse, in November 1993 the Food and Drug Administration (FDA) approved a controversial, genetically engineered version of a naturally occurring growth regulator called BGH, or bovine growth hormone. BGH boosts milk production in cows by 10 to 25 percent but also has sparked an intense health debate among scientists, consumer advocates and the dairy industry.

"This... hormone makes absolutely no sense for anyone other than the chemical and pharmaceutical companies that are trying to push this drug," warns Jeremy Rifkin, president of the Pure Food Campaign. Although extensive tests conducted by the companies show BGH poses no threat to humans, the campaign believes BGH is harmful to humans as well as cows and also threatens to put small dairy farmers out of business. They're not alone. A growing number of authorities say the safety studies — some of which haven't been made public — are inadequate and misleading.

"The FDA is skewing data and withholding critical information . . . regarding the safety of" BGH, charges Consumers Union, publisher of *Consumer Reports.* In fact, some studies show BGH could worsen udder infection rates in cows by up to 50 percent, increasing farmers' use of antibiotics. "This, in turn, would increase the risk of dangerous antibiotic residues in milk, posing a human health hazard," says Michael Hanson, Ph.D., a research associate for the organization. It also means that milk from BGH-treated cows would contain more pus and bacteria than regular milk, he adds.

In addition to those problems, BGH causes cattle to secrete extra amounts of a hormone called IGF-1, which has been linked to giantism in humans, according to Consumers Union. And union researchers believe it could indirectly contribute to the spread of a frightening group of degenerative diseases affecting the brains and nervous systems in animals and humans called transmissible spongiform encephalopathies. An outbreak of the disease appeared in 1985 in England, where it's known as "mad cow disease" because the animals become nervous and aggressive before dying. More than 80,000 cows have fallen prey to the illness, with nearly 900 new cases being diagnosed a week. Although some researchers believe the disease can't spread from animals to humans, many scientists maintain the evidence is unclear.

Tens of thousands of U.S. dairy farmers and processors oppose the use of BGH. They worry the genetically engineered drug could deal their business a knockout punch by reducing consumer demand at the same time it worsens the nation's milk glut. "We will not be silent as our livelihood is undermined by a drug, BGH, which neither we nor our consumers, nor our cows, want," says John Kinsman, a dairy farmer in LaValle, Wis.

Scores of dairy companies, responding to consumer concerns, already have pledged not to use milk or dairy products made with BGH. "We've been producing what I think is the best milk right up here in Sonoma and Marin counties for 16 years, and until the consumer tells me they want another product, I'm not going to change anything," Clover-Stornetta President Dan Benedetti says of his company's decision. Gary Hirshberg, president of Stonyfield Farm, says he fears BGH will ruin the integrity of

> ## Fish Oils Promote Health
>
> **Researchers have known for years that there's a connection between eating fish and reduced rates of cardiovascular disease. The reason may be that most fish is naturally low in fat, especially the heart-clogging saturated fat and cholesterol found in red meat. It's also high in Omega-3 unsaturated fatty acids, which help thin the blood and reduce cholesterol.**

the milk supply and destroy milk's good image among consumers.

As Rifkin notes: "BGH is bad for cows because it makes them sick. It's bad for consumers because drug residues will end up in our milk. It's bad for dairy farmers and will drive thousands of them out of business. And it's bad for taxpayers, who will have to pay hundreds of millions of dollars every year to buy up the surplus milk."

Despite such concerns, milk produced using BGH was expected to hit store shelves by early 1994. Labeling won't be required, partly because there's no way to test for the presence of the genetically engineered version of BGH.

The best way to ensure that the dairy products you buy are as pure as possible is to shop at natural products stores. Thousands of natural products manufacturers and retailers have pledged not to sell dairy products made with BGH (for a list of companies, contact: The Pure Food Campaign, 1130 17th St., N.W., Suite #300, Washington, D.C. 20036, 202-775-1132).

But remember that what's true for dairy products is also true for other beef, poultry and fish products. About 80 percent of all U.S. cattle, for instance, are implanted with hormones, according to the National Cattlemen's Association. If you want to be certain you're buying the purest meats possible, buy certified organic meats. Certified organic producers use extensive tracking systems to prove that their animals are raised, processed and packaged without the use of questionable antibiotics, growth hormones or additives.

Irradiation Approved by USDA

Irradiated poultry is now being sold in some areas of the country, much to the chagrin of many consumer advocates and health experts.

The U.S. Department of Agriculture (USDA) approved poultry irradiation in 1992, mostly to help combat increased outbreaks of salmonella poisoning, a bacterial infection that affects some 45,000 people a year. Irradiation kills salmonella bacteria without leaving the chicken radioactive. However, opponents argue that the radioactive material used to do it poses an environmental threat. And some health experts believe it may chemically alter food in a way that robs it of its nutrition and makes it carcinogenic.

"The only good irradiation does is to sanitize a filthy condition (of some poultry farms) by substituting it with a toxic one," says Michael Colby, national director of Food & Water Inc., a nonprofit food safety organization based in New York City.

Irradiated poultry doesn't have to be labeled if it's processed or packaged (in a TV dinner, for example), so the best assurance consumers have of avoiding it is to buy their organic and natural poultry from natural products manufacturers and retailers, who have widely pledged not to sell irradiated foods.

ENVIRONMENTAL REASONS TO BUY NATURAL MEATS & DAIRY PRODUCTS

Natural products retailers led the movement for dolphin-safe tuna and shrimp harvesting, but their widespread support of organic agriculture takes their commitment to humane farming practices a step farther. Farm animals receive much better treatment when they're raised organically rather than conventionally.

To begin with, certified organic farmers thoroughly inspect everything in their animals' environment to ensure it's truly organic — feed crops, grazing lands, supplemental feeds, even the water they drink — so they get the best of everything. To avoid the use of antibiotics, organic farmers also go to great lengths to keep their animals healthy. That means giving the animals plenty of room to range outdoors as well as making sure they have clean, roomy, well-lighted and well-ventilated cages or stalls that reduce stress and help prevent the spread of disease. It also means watching the animals closely for signs of illness. It takes one person to supervise 30 cows on the farms belonging to the Organic Valley dairy cooperative in Wisconsin, for instance, whereas up to 1,000 cows can be watched by one person on a crowded conventional farm.

Shunning antibiotics and other drugs can improve animals' lives in other ways, too. For instance, using genetically engineered BGH to increase milk production in dairy cows not only increases udder infections, it's also "like taking your cow and running it at 90 miles per hour all the time," says Mark Retzloff, president of Natural Horizons, a manufacturer of organic dairy foods in Boulder, Colo. "The cow's system is not made to do that. It puts the cow under stress... and the cow may not live as long."

ECONOMIC REASONS TO BUY NATURAL MEATS & DAIRY PRODUCTS

When we go grocery shopping, we choose whether or not to buy into the conglomerate agriculture system. "We must look at food in terms of the whole system—its relationship to the human body and its environmental impacts," says Fred Kirschenmann, Ph.D., president of the Organic Food Producers Association of North America. "When you buy an apple, you're supporting trees, soil and oxygen. When you buy a Twinkie, you're supporting a megacorporation. Large centralized food systems concentrating on mass production take away our freedom of choice. If we lose the choice to buy the foods we want, we'll lose our environmental and animal welfare agendas as well."

Shopping at a natural foods store helps register a consumer vote for organic fruits and vegetables and humanely produced meats and dairy products. Even this simple choice bucks the trend toward mass production.

For example, chickens were once free-range birds, scratching the soil for grubs, earthworms, grass and larvae. A rooster crowing at the break of day was a familiar sound. Now a $16 billion-a-year chicken industry controls every aspect of chicken production from feed mills to hatcheries to processing plants. In 1960, 286 companies sold commercially raised chickens to retail markets. Today, there are fewer than 50. These chicken "farms" are really "factories." Chickens live their entire lives inside windowless buildings surrounded by assembly lines, conveyer belts and fluorescent lights.

How to buy natural meat, seafood & poultry

There's no difference between cuts of meat in conventional and natural products stores (with the possible exception that full-service health food stores often offer a wider selection of gourmet meats and pre-prepared dishes). However, don't be surprised if natural meats are leaner, fresher and better tasting than their conventional counterparts because they're generally raised with little or no farm chemicals and drugs. Often, you'll also be able to find out more about where the meat came from and how it was prepared, since many natural foods retailers buy locally from farmers they know and trust and pay careful attention to how their other vendors do business.

The USDA does allow farmers to use an "all-natural" label. Technically, the label doesn't mean very much: only that natural meats have no artificial ingredients and are minimally processed, a standard that could apply to virtually all beef and chicken produced in the United States. In practice, the all-natural label often implies that meat or poultry is hormone-, antibiotic- and steroid free, a claim that's difficult — if not impossible — to verify with testing but easier to corroborate if you can find out how the animal was raised. Similar problems afflict the use of marketing terms such as "hormone free," "antibiotic free" and "free-range." Antibiotic free, for example, might mean a turkey was given antibiotics as a chick, when birds are more susceptible to disease, then left untreated for the remainder of its life. It may or may not have been tested for the presence of unacceptable levels of antibiotic residues after its slaughter.

Fish and seafood raise a whole new set of issues. If fish are taken from oceans or rivers, it's virtually impossible to determine what they've been exposed to during their lifetimes, including pesticide runoff, illegally dumped toxic wastes and oil spills. Many natural products retailers combat this problem by buying fresh fish from vendors they trust, inspecting it personally and sometimes testing it randomly to avoid fish that's been treated with salts or preservatives. Some buy shellfish from dealers who have been certified by the Interstate Shellfish Sanitation Conference, which monitors certain waters for contaminants. Other retailers refuse to buy fish and seafood from certain waters — the polluted Great Lakes, for example. Farm-raised, grain-fed shrimp, trout, salmon, catfish and other fish often are a known quantity, may have been fed organic grain and make healthy alternatives to wild species.

✺

Chapter 7
SOYFOODS

How To Shop For Meat & Dairy Alternatives

HOW SOYFOODS ARE MADE

There's something unusual happening in the dairy case at your local natural foods store. In addition to the usual assortment of milk, eggs and cheese, the shelves are lined with boxes of tofu, packages of tempeh and cartons of soy milk.

Many of these products are designed to look and taste like their conventional counterparts — mozzarella cheese, yogurt, hot dogs, and variations of them are spilling over into other aisles. Soy-based ice creams, chocolates and micowaveable dinners are among the soyfood choices now available to shoppers. Most are better for your health and the environment than foods made with meat and dairy products, yet they remain a mystery to many consumers. How are these versatile and economical foods made? Here's a quick guide to the basics:

Tofu — A mainstay in the Orient for at least 2,000 years, tofu is the curd that results when the juice of cooked soybeans is coagulated and pressed into cubes. High in protein, calcium, iron, B vitamins and vitamin E, it's relatively low in calories and very low in saturated fat (it derives 30 to 40 percent of its calories from fat, however, and shouldn't be mistaken for a low-fat food even though it compares favorably to meat). Fresh tofu tastes similar to pasta but becomes almost flavorless once it's packaged, assuming the flavor of whatever's added to it. There are several textures of tofu. They include silken, which has a soft consistency and can be scrambled like eggs or used to make desserts, and extra firm, which is meatier and useful for stir-frying. Tofu also is flavored and formed using modern technology into more familiar shapes — hot dogs and lunch meat, for instance. Soy milk, a staple food in the Orient, is almost always flavored in the United States to hide its beany taste. It's often available in a variety of flavors, from plain — which tastes like whole milk — to almond and cocoa. It's also used to make cheeses (which may contain enzymes, or casein, from cows), yogurts and other dairy look-alikes.

Tempeh—Tempeh is made from cracked whole soybeans that are cooked, fermented and steamed. It originated several hundred years ago in Indonesia and is about 20 percent protein. Slightly sour in taste, tempeh is like meat and generally ranges from creamy white to pale yellow in color, although it can turn almost black during fermentation. Many meat substitutes are made from tempeh, including bacon and burgers. Although many people enjoy tempeh plain, the addition of familiar flavors such as barbecue sauce and lemon juice make it more palatable to most Americans.

Textured Vegetable Protein (TVP)—Americans have been eating TVP for years without knowing it because versions of it frequently are added to foods to boost their protein content. TVP is made from soy flour after the soybean oil has been extracted, and it's sold in granules, flakes, chunks and slices. It has no cholesterol, is low in sodium and has almost no fat, but it can be cooked like hamburger and added to chili, spaghetti sauce and sloppy joes. It also can be combined with other ingredients or shaped into patties.

Seitan—Seitan originated thousands of years ago in the Orient, where it was made from whole wheat, tamari (a type of soy sauce) and spices. The dough is continually kneaded and rinsed until it becomes glutinous (thick and sticky), then shaped into any form and cooked in a flavorful broth. High in protein, seitan contains no cholesterol but has the consistency and flavor of meat — so much so that some dedicated vegetarians refuse to eat it. Seitan is often used in tacos, stroganoff, meatballs, stir-fries and meatloaf. Many manufacturers also make seitan steaks and sliced lunch meats.

ENVIRONMENTAL REASONS TO BUY SOYFOODS

Many experts believe the environment might be the biggest benefactor of a worldwide conversion to a plant-based diet rich in fruits, vegetables and soyfoods.

Environmentalist John Robbins, son of the founder of Baskin-Robbins ice cream, points out that it takes 16 pounds of grain to produce a pound of beef. That means that if Americans reduced their yearly meat consumption by only 10 percent, enough grain would be saved to feed 60 million people, he says. And because it takes less land to feed a person on a plant-based diet than it does to feed a meat eater, cutting back also would benefit our natural resources.

"In almost every country in the world more and more forests are being cut down to clear land to grow cattle feed or to graze cattle," Robbins says, noting that 64 percent of U.S. cropland is devoted to producing livestock feed, compared to 2 percent for growing fruits and vegetables. Worldwide, half the Earth's landmass is grazed by livestock, he says. "Prairies, grasslands and rangelands are destroyed by the overgrazing of livestock. As we shift to a plant-based diet, much of the land that has been deforested can be returned to forests, which will provide forestry jobs, tourism and ecological benefits such as holding topsoil, providing habitats for wildlife, providing oxygen to the atmosphere and extracting carbon dioxide."

Adds Robbins: "A reduction in meat consumption may well be the most potent single act we can take to halt destruction of our environment and preserve our precious natural resources."

HEALTH REASONS TO EAT SOYFOODS

Can a plant-based diet provide you with enough nutrition, including protein? The answer is a resounding yes, especially when soyfoods are eaten.

The Recommended Daily Allowance (RDA) of protein is about .36 grams of protein per pound of body weight — about 58 grams a day for a 160-pound man, 43 grams for a 120-pound woman. Many experts believe Americans eat about twice as much protein as they need, most of it from meat and dairy foods that are high in fat, calories and cholesterol. The average cholesterol count of people who eat a meat-centered diet is 210 mg./dl., a level that increases the average male's chances of dying from heart disease to more than 50 percent. And since protein can't be stored by the body, the kidneys and liver must strain to get rid of it. Perhaps it's no surprise that high protein consumption has been linked to kidney disease as well as cancers of the colon, breast, prostate and pancreas.

Complete proteins also are important to the diet. Foods that contain precise proportions of amino acids — the body's building blocks — are considered complete proteins. Meat, fish, eggs and dairy products provide them. Fruits and vegetables are usually incomplete, meaning they're abundant in some amino acids and lacking in others. One exception is soy protein, which is complete. Although some nutrition experts once thought vegetarians had to combine certain foods at each meal to get enough complete proteins, they now know differently. Amino acids that don't form a complete protein survive in the body for 12 hours — long enough for some nutritional processes to take place.

The U.S. Department of Agriculture has understood the benefits of reducing animal fat since 1971. That was the year the department estimated there could be a 38.8 percent reduction in the incidence of disease and a 34.2 percent reduction in medical costs if Americans cut their intake of animal fat and started eating more fiber, fruits and vegetables.

Soyfoods protect against cancer

Evidence is mounting that soyfoods can help prevent cancer. In Singapore, for example, an analysis of the eating habits of more than 600 women showed that those with the highest soyfoods consumption were half as likely to get breast cancer, says Mark Messina, Ph.D., a former top administrator at the Diet and Cancer Branch of the National Cancer Institute. Studies in Japan, China and the United States show that including tofu, soy milk and soy sprouts in the diet cuts the risk of colon and rectal cancer in half. In one study, eating soybeans and tofu reduced the risk of rectal cancer by 80 percent.

Soyfoods consumption also appears to lower the risk of stomach, lung and prostate cancer. In one study of more than 8,000 men of Japanese ancestry living in Hawaii, eating tofu lowered the risk of prostate cancer more than any other dietary factor studied.

Scientists believe the anticancer benefits of soyfoods are twofold. First, soyfoods tend to be lower in fat and are higher in fiber than meat. High-fat and low-fiber intake have been linked to cancer. Soyfoods also contain at least five compounds with anticancer properties including isoflavones. Soybeans are the only commonly consumed food containing isoflavones. In a 1989 study of rats with breast cancer, the rats who were fed a diet containing soybeans had about 50 percent fewer tumors. However, when they were fed soy minus its isoflavones, there was no effect on the tumors. Isoflavones may help explain why breast cancer rates are lower in countries such as Japan and China — where soybeans are an important part of the diet — than they are in Western countries.

(SOY)Milk's the one

Next time you start to pour a glass of milk, why not consider soy milk instead? Milk's health hazards are the subject of more and more warnings from physicians and other authorities. It was recently implicated as a trigger for insulin-dependent diabetes by famed baby doctor Benjamin Spock, M.D., as well as Frank Oski, M.D., director of pediatrics at Johns Hopkins University, and Neal Barnard, M.D., president of the Physicians Committee for Responsible Medicine. Meanwhile, a recent congressional report maintains that the public isn't being protected from dangerous drug residues found in the nation's milk supply. It's also been fingered as the culprit in allergy and digestive problems, particularly among African-Americans and Asians who lack the enzyme required to digest the milk sugar, lactose.

Given that milk also contains significant amounts of fat, saturated fat and cholesterol, which contribute to cardiovascular disease and certain forms of cancer, and that many other foods — including soy milk — are rich sources of calcium, soy milk becomes appealing.

Four Terrific Reasons to Eat Soyfoods

1. They're nutritious
Soybeans are a high-yield protein source. Per acre, soybean crops provide 15 times more protein than animal sources. They're also rich in calcium, iron, B vitamins and vitamin E. Plus, they're lower in fat than meat and dairy foods. Soy fiber has been shown to stabilize blood sugar levels and regulate blood pressure. Studies also show that soyfoods help prevent certain forms of cancer.

2. They're ecological
Because soybeans grow close to the ground, they crowd out weeds, eliminating the need for herbicides. They're also highly pest resistant, decreasing the need for pesticides. Protein for protein, soybeans use 200 percent less water than cattle, requiring little or no irrigation. Plus, they add natural nitrogen to the soil, which is one reason why farmers use them as a rotation crop.

3. They're economical
Soybeans are an economically sound way to add protein to the diet. One acre of land devoted to soy will produce enough food to meet an individual's protein requirements for more than 2,000 days. An acre dedicated to beef production nets enough protein for only 77 days.

4. They're versatile
Tofu, tempeh and textured vegetable protein (TVP) make great replacements for meat in soups, casseroles and most other dishes. Soy milk and cheese are lactose-free alternatives to cow or goat milk on cereal or in baked goods.

Healthy Grilling with Soyfoods
Tofu and tempeh are great-tasting, healthier alternatives to meat when it comes to barbecuing. Grilled meat contains potent mutagens called heterocyclic aromatic amines (HAAs), which can initiate cancer-producing changes in our body's DNA. HAAs are created when amino acids and creatinine, both present in meat, are heated together at temperatures exceeding 212 degrees Fahrenheit. Most barbecues are hotter than 350 degrees Fahrenheit.

However, soyfoods don't contain creatinine and therefore don't form HAAs when they're grilled, according to John Weisburger, Ph.D., of the American Health Foundation.

Chapter 8
HOUSEHOLD GOODS

How To Buy Environmental Household Goods

HEALTH REASONS TO USE ECOLOGICAL HOUSEHOLD PRODUCTS

Your great-grandmother didn't need a closet full of toxic chemicals to clean her home, and you don't either. Today's natural products stores feature the latest in a rapidly growing line of environmentally friendly cleaning products, ranging from unbleached paper towels to nonpolluting laundry detergents.

It's difficult to gauge what impact conventional household cleaners have on our lives, but the signs aren't good. Modern cleaning products are packed with powerful petrochemicals, disinfectants, phosphates and detergents that can harm our health. In fact, more than 70,000 new chemical compounds have been introduced into the environment in the past 25 years. Even when used according to directions, many cleaners, air fresheners and aerosol sprays contain large amounts of volatile organic compounds that evaporate easily, polluting the air for days after use. Children are more vulnerable than adults to the chemicals because they breathe in more air relative to their body size, may absorb toxins more quickly because their skin is thinner, and their bodies are less able to break down toxic substances, says Charity Vitale, Ph.D., co-author of *Healthy Homes, Healthy Kids*.

Among other things, many scientists believe household chemicals are a likely contributor to allergies, which are 10 times higher today than they were in the 1960s for adults and 20 times higher for children. Most people spend 90 percent of their time indoors, mostly in their own homes. Unfortunately, because of our reliance on chemical cleaners, that's also where you'll find the nation's worst air pollution, according to a 1989 report by the Environmental Protection Agency. Hazardous and toxic chemicals course through the typical American home at concentrations two to five times higher than levels outdoors, often making the air inside our homes more dangerous than it is in our inner cities.

To make matters worse, some household chemicals are suspected carcinogens that might not be clearly labeled. For example, methylene chloride, a suspected carginogen, is used in wood stains, varnishes, water repellant and spray paint yet seldom appears on labels or is termed "chlorinated solvent" or "aromatic hydrocarbon."

According to *Healthy Homes, Healthy Kids*, common household chemicals that can be harmful include:

Ammonia
Used in disinfectants and window cleaners, it can burn the skin and irritate the eyes and lungs. Combined with chlorine bleach, it forms deadly chloramine gas.

Chlorinated phenols
Found in toilet bowl cleaners, they're toxic to the respiratory and circulatory systems.

Diethylene glycol
An ingredient of window cleaners, floor cleaners and waxes, it depresses the central nervous system.

Formaldehyde
Used in spray and wick deodorizers, it can cause respiratory irritation, nausea, headaches and shortness of breath. It's also a suspected carcinogen.

Hydrochloric acid
Found in drain openers and toilet bowl cleaners, it burns the skin and irritates the nose and lungs.

Perchloroethylene
An ingredient of spot removers, it causes liver and kidney damage.

Petroleum solvents
Used in floor cleaners and waxes, they irritate the skin, eyes, nose and lungs.

Petroleum distillates
Found in furniture polish, they irritate the skin, eyes, nose, throat and lungs.

Phenols
An ingredient of disinfectants, they're toxic to the respiratory and circulatory systems.

Potassium hydroxide (lye)
Used in oven cleaners, it burns the skin and irritates the eyes.

Sodium hydroxide (lye)
Found in drain cleaners, it burns the skin and eyes and irritates the lungs.

Sodium hypochlorites
Ingredients of disinfectants, bleach and spot removers, they burn the skin and irritate the lungs.

Trichloromethane (a petroleum distillate)
Used in drain cleaners, it irritates the nose and eyes, depresses the central nervous system (causing drowsiness or dizziness) and increases the frequency of cellular mutation.

ENVIRONMENTAL REASONS TO BUY ECOLOGICAL HOUSEHOLD PRODUCTS

All cleaning products impact the environment in some way, but the key is to minimize their use and rely on products containing more benign ingredients. Here's a guide to some of the ingredients natural products industry experts say consumers should be concerned about when buying household goods:

Chlorine bleaches
Mostly found in the form of sodium hypochlorite, bleaches can lead to the formation of dioxins in the environment.

EDTA (Ethylene diaminotetra acetate)
EDTA can attach to metals such as lead or mercury in sediment and mobilize them back into the water supply. It's also less biodegradable than NTA.

Enzymes
These agents break down proteins such as chocolate. Because human skin also is protein, enzymes can irritate the skin.

NTA (Nitrilotriacetic acid)
Banned in some European countries, NTA biodegrades slowly in cold environments and combines with heavy metals such as lead, bringing harmful compounds back into the water supply.

Nonyl phenol ethoxylate
This surfactant biodegrades slowly, and some experts believe it may break down into even more toxic compounds.

Optical brighteners
Brighteners can cause allergic reactions, restrict bacteria growth and cause mutations in bacteria. Although they break down quickly in smaller particles, they may resist biodegrading further.

Petroleum-based surfactants
Commonly listed on labels as detergents, these cleaning agents are derived wholly from nonrenewable petroleum resources and, during biodegradation, can form compounds containing cancer-causing chemicals, some more harmful than the surfactant itself.

Phosphates
These plant nutrients are used in cleaning products to soften water. However, they also feed algae in waterways, reducing oxygen supplies and suffocating fish. Phosphates also may be related to the presence of arsenic in laundry detergents, according to a 1990 report by the Washington Toxics Coalition.

Polycarboxylates
Sometimes substituted for phosphates, these agents are derived from petrochemicals and biodegrade slowly, if at all.

Preservatives
Some such as formaldehyde are barely biodegradable. They may also be toxic or cancer causing.

How to Buy Ecological Household Products

Most everyone wants to use environmentally friendly products these days, but it's not always clear what "environmentally friendly" or other green marketing terms mean because there are no national standards governing their use.

So how do consumers make buying decisions when it comes to household products? Industry experts recommend avoiding products that make general claims such as "biodegradable" unless specific ingredients and their functions are also listed on their labels. The more specific the label, the better it is. For example, stating that a product contains fragrance is vague, whereas explaining that the fragrance is citrus oil is more specific. In addition, make sure the listing is an ingredient, not a description such as "organic biodegradable surfactant." Surfactants may be petroleum- or vegetable based. A perfect label lists the chemical names of its ingredients and then explains what the chemical is for and how it's derived.

No matter how good a product's label is, however, consumers are likely to be faced with difficult — sometimes confusing — choices when it comes to buying environmental household products. Biodegradability, for example, is rarely a clear-cut issue. Ideally, biodegradation means the complete breakdown of a product into carbon dioxide, water and minerals. Often, however, it's measured experimentally by looking only for the disappearance of the parent compound, which might not be best for the environment. Some ingredients will break down into fairly large particles within 24 hours, for instance, then go no further for many years. Others may break down quickly yet initially can be more harmful to the environment. Some take longer to biodegrade in cold weather than in warm weather, while others become even more toxic by combining with other compounds.

Generally, environmental experts say shoppers should look for products that are:

- **Petroleum free.**
- **Biodegradable.**
- **Phosphate free.**
- **Chlorine free.**
- **Free of synthetic dyes, perfumes and coloring agents.**

But it's also important to search for products that:

- **Release no persistent toxins into the environment during production, use or disposal.**
- **Are made from recycled material or renewable resources extracted in a way that doesn't harm the environment.**
- **Are made to be durable and reusable first, or recyclable and truly biodegradable second.**
- **Are minimally packaged.**
- **Include information about the manufacturer, including location, labor practices and additional products or businesses.**

INDEX

Acacia, **34**
Acidophilus, **16**
Algae extracts, **29**
Allantoin, **32**
Allium cepa, **25**
Aloe vera, **29**
Amazake, **55**
American ginseng, **19, 22**
Antibiotic free, **62**
Antioxidants, **10, 11, 40**
Apis mellifica, **25**
Arnica, **25, 26, 34**
Aromatherapy, **24**
Arsenicum album, **25**
Astragalus, **21, 22**
Azulene, **32**
Barley malt, **55**
Belladonna, **25**
Beneficial bacteria, **16**
Bergamot, **24**
Beta-carotene, **12, 14, 17, 40**
Betaine, **31, 34**
Bifidobacteria, **16**
Birch, **34**
Borage oil, **28**
Bovine growth hormone (BGH), **58, 59, 60, 61**
Brown rice syrup, **56**
Bryonia, **25**
Calcium, **13, 15, 17, 32, 49, 63, 67**
Calendula salve, **27**
Canola oil, **54**
Cantharis, **25**
Carotene, **13**
Cayenne, **26**
Chamomile, **22, 24, 32, 34**
Chamomilla, **25**
Chaste berry, **23**
Chlorine free, **71**
Chromium, **10**
Citric acid, **32**
Clary sage, **24**
Clover, **34**
Cocoa butter, **29**
Coconut oil, **29, 31**
Cold-pressed oils, **54**
Comfrey, **27, 32**
Complete proteins, **65**
Copper, **10, 32, 40**
Corn syrup, **56**
Cress, **40**

Date syrup, **56**
Diffuser, **24**
Dong Quai, **23**
Echinacea, **19, 21, 26**
Ephedra, **23**
Eucalyptus, **24**
Evening primrose oil, **29**
Expeller-pressed oils, **54**
Eyebright, **23**
Fish oil, **59**
Flax oil, **54**
Flower remedies, **26**
Folic acid, **14, 17**
Free range, **62**
Fructose, **56**
Garlic, **18, 19**
Genetic engineering, **37, 42, 58-61**
Ginger, **26, 34**
Ginkgo biloba, **18**
Ginseng, **21, 34**
Glucose glutamate, **34**
Goldenseal, **19, 21, 34**
Gotu kola, **21**
Grape seed oil, **29**
Grindelia, **26**
Glycerin, **29**
Henna, **34**
Ho-shou-wu, **21**
Homeopathy, **25**
Honey, **56**
Hops, **22, 34**
Hormone free, **62**
Horsetail, **31, 34**
Hydrogenation, **54**
Ignatia, **25**
Iodine, **32**
Ipecac, syrup of, **26**
Iron, **13, 15, 17, 32, 40, 49, 63, 67**
Irradiated, **37, 42, 60**
Isoflavones, **66**
Jasmine, **24**
Jojoba oil, **24, 28, 29, 31**
Juniper, **34**
Kelp, **32**
Lachesis, **25**
Lactobacillus, **16**
Lavender, **24, 31**
Lecithin, **29, 31**
Licorice, **18, 21**

Magnesium, **13, 15, 17, 32**
Mag phos, **25**
Manganese, **10, 17, 40**
Mannitol, **56**
Maple syrup, **56**
Minerals, **13, 32**
Mint, **32, 34**
Molasses, **57**
Multivitamins, **13**
Nettles, **23, 31, 34**
Niacin, **12, 14**
Nux vomica, **25**
Olive oil, **31, 34, 54**
Omega-3 fatty acids, **54**
Organic meats, **60, 62**
Palm kernel oil, **31**
Panthenol, **34**
Pantothenic acid, **15**
Passion flower, **22**
Peppermint, **24, 27**
Phosphate free, **71**
Phosphorus **32, 49**
Poppy, **26**
Potassium, **32, 49**
Poultice powder, **27**
Pulsatilla, **25**
Pyridoxine, **12, 14, 17**
Rasberry leaf, **23**
Rhus tox, **25**
Riboflavin, **14**
Rice bran oil, **29, 54**
Rose, **24**
Rosemary, **24, 31, 34**
Safflower oil, **29, 54**
Sage, **31, 34**
Salicylic acid, **32**
Sandalwood, **24**
Schizandra, **21**
Seaweed, **29**
Selenium, **10-13, 17, 40**
Selenomethionine, **13**
Sepia, **25**
Shea butter, **29**
Shiitake, **22**
Siberian ginseng, **21, 22, 23**
Slippery elm, **27**
Sodium, **32**
Sorbitol, **57**
Sorghum molasses, **57**

Soy milk, **63, 66, 67**
Soy oil, **54**
Soyfoods, **63, 64, 65, 66**
Spearmint, **24**
Squalene oil, **29**
St. John's wort, **22**
Steroid free, **62**
Stevia leaf, **57**
Sucanat, **57**
Sulphur, **25**
Suma, **21**
Sunflower oil, **28, 29**
Sweet almond oil, **31**
Tamari, **64**
Tannin, **32**
Tea tree, **24, 27, 34**
Tempeh, **46, 63, 64, 67**
Textured vegetable protein (TVP), **64, 67**
Thiamine, **14, 42**
Tinctures, **20**
Tofu, **46, 50, 63, 66, 67**
Turbinado sugar, **57**
Unrefined oils, **54**
Valerian, **22, 26**
Vitamin A, **10, 13, 14, 32, 49**
Vitamin B, **13, 32, 49, 63, 67**
Vitamin B Complex, **13, 32**
Vitamin B-1, **14, 42**
Vitamin B-2, **14**
Vitamin B-3, **12, 14**
Vitamin B-6, **12, 14, 17**
Vitamin B-9, **14, 17**
Vitamin B-12, **32**
Vitamin C, **10-13, 15, 32, 49**
Vitamin D, **13, 15, 32**
Vitamin E, **12, 13, 15, 32, 63, 67**
Vitamin K, **32**
Wheat germ oil, **29, 34**
Wines, organic, **36**
Xylitol, **57**
Yarrow, **34**
Ylang ylang, **24**
Zinc, **10, 12, 15, 17, 34**